Cornell Industrial and Labor Relations Bibliography Series
No. 16

374
62

Academic Women and Employment Discrimination
A Critical Annotated Bibliography

Jennie Farley

New York State School of
Industrial and Labor Relations
Cornell University

Cover design by Michael Rider

Library of Congress number: 82-3570
ISBN: 0-87546-092-5

Cataloging in Publication Data

Farley, Jennie.
  Academic women and employment discrimination.

  (Cornell industrial and labor relations
bibliography series; no. 16)
    1. Women college teachers—United States—
Abstracts.   2. Sex discrimination against women—
United States—Abstracts.   3. Women college
teachers—Employment—United States—Abstracts.
I. Title.   II. Series.
  LB2332.3.F37   016.378'12'088042   82-3570
  ISBN 0-87546-092-5 (pbk.)   AACR2

Copies may be ordered from
ILR Publications
New York State School of
Industrial and Labor Relations
Cornell University
Ithaca, NY 14853

Contents

Introduction

This bibliography attempts to draw together sources of information about sex discrimination in higher education and efforts to eliminate it. It grew out of a conference entitled Creative Approaches to Ending Sex Discrimination in Higher Education, which focused on the need for reform in faculty recruitment, selection, promotion, and grievance handling. The conference had made clear that there were information gaps. While some present were well informed about social science research documenting the extent of sex discrimination on American campuses, others had no idea that such studies had been done. Some participants were knowledgeable about lawsuits charging sex discrimination that had gone to court in the 1970s and how they had been resolved by judges; others clearly did not know details of the cases and wanted to. Still others were familiar with policy reforms and innovations being instituted by imaginative academic administrators, faculty members, and affirmative action officers, while others, thinking that universities considered their personnel policies cast in concrete, were astonished to hear about them. This bibliography attempts to draw attention to the best sources of information on these topics.

Most of the items reviewed here have appeared since 1970. A few researchers (e.g., Bernard 1964) had assessed academic women's problems earlier, but most of the publishing activity came in the 1970s. In the early part of the decade, the emphasis was on documenting the problem. On 125 campuses, groups of women prepared reports and calls for action, using statistics that showed women professors to be few and far between. Their methodology was to be questioned later (Lester 1977), as was their objectivity. Using that evidence, women's groups argued that the Civil Rights Act of 1964 be extended to women (Harris 1970), and it was. Then came a spate of writing on ways in which the law should be implemented and, later, on why it was not succeeding. In the late 1970s, the writing focused either on why affirmative action was not needed or on the lawsuits filed by women academics who found that despite ten years of lip service to academic affirmative action, nothing had changed (Abramson 1979).

More than half the items cited are from professional journals from a variety of disciplines: law, sociology, psychology, education, economics, business. About a third of the entries are books: law handbooks; reports of commissions, associations, foundations, and women's organizations; collections of papers; proceedings of conferences. The remaining items are diverse: articles from newspapers, newsletters, periodicals, summaries of students' observations and surveys. Alumni monthlies proved to be authoritative sources. These magazines are not house organs in the usual sense. The editors appear to be relatively independent of institutional control and take extraordinary pains to present in satisfying detail not only the institution's version of what transpired in a given case but the perspective of the plaintiff as well. Almost all the research reported here was undertaken on college and university campuses, but some studies were done in industry. These are included because their findings have clear implications for academics.

Most of the material from professional journals is accessible to the general reader, but sometimes specialists do tend to talk to one another in private language. Attorneys often refer to a principle established in a case by the plaintiff's name, e.g., "Using *Griggs* . . . " or "*Sweeney* and its progeny. . . . " On the other hand, they, unlike some social scientists, are careful to document every assertion they make with a flurry of *ibid.*'s and *supra*s. Economists sometimes present elaborate regressions and statistical test results without defining their terms in enough detail so that the noneconomist can know what they were purporting to measure. Educators describe grievances on their campuses with allusions to practices that are puzzling even to other educators. Because, for instance, associate professors usually have tenure on one campus, it does not necessarily follow that they do elsewhere; or since instructors are ineligible for tenure at one institution, this is not necessarily so at others.

Of the 179 items included in this bibliography, 17 are anonymous reports of commissions, associations' policy statements, articles in law reviews, and the like. Of the 207 authors and editors listed, 8 could not be identified by sex either because they used initials or because they have names used by both sexes. Of the remaining 199 authors, two-thirds are women. Issues of sex discrimination appear to be of more concern to women academics than to men. To be sure, most grievants in sex discrimination suits against universities are women, while most educational administrators, tenured faculty members, and judges are not.

The recommendations for policy change in the works cited here should be interpreted, of course, in terms of how those who suggested them defined the issue. Economists often approach these problems as ones of measurement. They may identify a pay gap between the average salaries of men and women at an institution and seek to account for it by comparing other characteristics of the subjects. If they explain away 75 percent of the variation, they may then conclude that the rest is due to unknown factors, one of which may be discrimination. Experimental social scientists attack the issue differently. In a typical study, the researcher sends out descriptions of ten individuals to department chairpersons, asking them to evaluate these candidates' suitability for jobs. What the chairpersons do not know is that the sex of the individuals has been varied by the experimenter, to see if identical credentials were judged differently if they were thought to have been earned by women rather than by men (Fidell 1970).

Of course, the same evidence can be perceived differently by different observers. Three sociologists (Wolfe, LeFleur, and Slocum 1973) study the status of women in their discipline and conclude that since only a quarter of the sociology doctorates are being awarded to women, recruitment of more women graduate students is what requires the most attention. In the rejoinder to their article in the *American Sociologist*, women's caucus representatives note that fully a quarter of the doctorates are being earned by women, but of those Ph.D. holders, fewer than half are being hired to tenure-track faculty posts. Therefore, they say, before more women are recruited into graduate school, the hiring practices need attention.

The reader can find other examples of differing interpretations of the same evidence here:

> Knoll (1977) reviews legal decisions that suggest that the courts should not interfere with the employment decisions of private universities; a lengthy note in the *Harvard Law Review* ("Academic Freedom . . . " 1979) affirms the constitutionality of such interference.

> A Montana State administrator (Clark 1977) reports that the consent decree signed there satisfied both the institution and the

grievants; one of the plaintiffs is reported to have found it far less satisfactory (Abramson 1979).

A commentator in the *Labor Law Journal* (Foegen 1979) opines that being a woman is a definite asset in job hunting in the 1970s; an economist (Baldwin 1979) counters with the fact of continuing labor market discrimination against women and blacks.

A department chairman reports at an annual meeting that the low status of women in English departments is due to their life choices; the women present review his data and find his conclusion unsupported (Gleason 1971).

Hill analyzes the structure and function of the Equal Employment Opportunity Commission (1977); one wonders how, with so little support from Congress and the executive offices, the EEOC ever got anything done. But Haber (1981) points out that a determined and talented EEOC investigator was what made it possible for a woman to begin to get justice at Berkeley.

Aiken (1976) comments approvingly that judges are keeping hands off university personnel policies; Johnson and Knapp (1971) review a century of judicial decisions and conclude that the sexism on the bench is perpetuating sex discrimination.

A former college president reviews the case at the University of Georgia where assistant professor Maija Blaubergs was denied tenure and sued. One of her colleagues went to jail in his academic robes rather than reveal how he had voted on her candidacy. Bunzel (1981) points out that the woman's credentials were reviewed by no fewer than nine university committees and invariably found wanting. Bolarsky (1980) writes that the controversy over secret ballots has obscured the real issue: the candidate was recommended for tenure no fewer than three times by her department colleagues, the very ones whose judgment is said to be decisive in academe.

The American Association of University Professors still maintains that grievance procedures should be concerned with the way in which decisions are made and not the merits of individual cases (AAUP 1977); the committee on women within the organization expresses concern for the rights of grievants (Francis 1981).

The Princeton University annual report of the president (1980) maintains that good progress is being made toward integrating the faculty by sex; a newspaper reporter (Remnick 1979) finds otherwise.

The status of women students in higher education is changing rapidly. Cornell University, a leader in this regard, has admitted women for more than a century. Other Ivy League institutions, which admitted only men in the past, opened their doors to women in the 1970s. Women now comprise well over a third of the students in the Ivy League, as can be seen from table 1. Two of the most distinguished women's colleges have changed markedly during the same period: Vassar began to admit men, and Radcliffe merged with Harvard.

Women's progress on the faculties at Ivy League institutions and at other colleges and universities has been painfully slow (table 1 also shows that men are much better represented on women's college faculties than women are on Ivy League faculties). In the 1970s, there was progress in appointments at the lecturer and assistant professor levels but little movement into the tenured ranks. Establishing their legal rights to challenge university personnel decisions was a slow process for academic women in the 1970s, as can be seen from the list of cases in table 2. This list is drawn in part from several works included in this bibliography (Flygare 1980–81; LaNoue 1981; Reeves 1977; Vladeck and Young 1978; and Yurko 1980), from the files of the Women's Equity Action League, Washington, D.C., and from legal briefs filed by both the plaintiffs and the defendant in Civil Action No. 80-CV-455, U.S. District Court, Northern District of New York, the case of *Zahorik et al. v. Cornell University*. Some of the cases were filed by males; they are included because they illustrate judicial thinking that has implications (mostly ominous ones) for women's future success in the courts.

Women's right to challenge academic personnel decisions has begun to be established in the courts. The studies and decisions chosen for this bibliography most clearly favor grievants and their supporters. One reason for this is that aggrieved academics are more likely to seek publicity and support than are defenders of institutions. Many entries suggest ways in which problems can be detected and prevented before they get to court. There are proposals for informal methods for resolving sexual harassment problems (Rowe 1981), proposals for grievance arbitration (McCarthy 1981); and publications that include self-study quizzes for administrators (Bogart 1980). A reader can measure his or her own institution by comparing it to others (*An Inventory . . .* 1980). An attorney proposes that a radically different way of viewing universities and colleges, in terms of their unique missions, might well bring more judicial objectivity in future sex discrimination cases (Yurko 1980).

But many of the recommendations for policy change reviewed here were formulated and published before the current ground swell of litigation. The American Association of University Professors and the Association of American Colleges (*Faculty Tenure,* 1973) foresaw trouble in institutions in which more than two-thirds of the faculty had tenure; a university ombudsman (Cook 1972) pinpointed the need for change in hiring practices since contemporary policies, while neutral on the surface, were clearly disadvantageous to women; and as early as 1964 the Massachusetts Institute of Technology was holding a conference on the problems faced by women in science and engineering, at which some of the participants focused on institutional policies and practices (Mattfeld and Van Aken 1965). The consent decrees signed, after protracted litigation, by Brown University and by the University of Minnesota were discussed at the conference that inspired this bibliography. Attorney Judith Vladeck observed that it was not, in her opinion, beyond the ingenuity of academics to improve their practices so as to avoid outside litigation. One observer, a former academic administrator, lamented the fact that the wheels of academic life grind exceedingly slowly. She said, "What we need to do on each American campus is to formulate our own consent decrees—without the help of the courts. If we don't, they'll do it for us." Others respond that the courts should not intervene, and will not, if institutional cases are presented with enough imagination and care. But to focus attention on managing liability, according to some administrators, is to ensure that more university money will be spent on expensive legal staff rather than on support of scholarship and teaching. As will be clear from a perusal of this bibliography and the sources it contains, defenders of universities and grievants alike find the government agencies woefully inadequate. Almost all concerned also find the costly and time-consuming litigation an unsatisfactory solution to a growing problem.

Despite ten years of litigation and a decade of affirmative action, women still face formidable obstacles in academic life. Students still rate courses they think will be offered by women lower than identical courses identified as taught by males (Kaschak 1978). Women Ph.D.'s in science can still look forward to lower pay and slower advancement than their male colleagues can (Ahern and Scott 1981). The idea that having more women as role models and mentors will help women students and junior staff appears to be more wishful thinking than a firm prediction based on evidence (Speizer 1981). Male academics persist in their belief that women won't fit in or don't belong in academic life (Guillemin 1979, George 1979). As one recent article shows, when a woman scholar complains that men are stealing the fruits of her research work, she may be told to stop complaining or she will lose her job (Hunt 1981). At the end of 1981, there were no fewer than 217 grievances filed by individual women scholars with federal and state agencies, in court, or both. Whatever else the 1980s will bring—from fewer academic posts for women or men in colleges and universities to dwindling commitment to affirmative action in Washington—it will surely bring more allegations of academic sex discrimination unless there is massive change on campus.

Table 1. Female Students and Faculty, Ivy League and Seven Sisters Institutions

	Women as Percentage of Undergraduate Student Body	Women as Percentage of Total Faculty
Ivy League		
Brown	47%	13%
Columbia[1]	0	16
Cornell	43	17[2]
Dartmouth	32	19
Harvard	37	11
University of Pennsylvania	38	15
Princeton	35	11
Yale	41	19
Seven Sisters		
Barnard	100	59
Bryn Mawr	100	49
Mount Holyoke	100	50
Radcliffe[3]	-	-
Smith	100	39
Vassar	60	39
Wellesley	100	54

Sources: *The Competitive Colleges* (Princeton, N.J.: Peterson's Guides, 1981), and *Academe* (Bulletin of the AAUP) 66 (September 1980): 287–307. Percentages from *Academe* have been rounded to the nearest whole percentage point.

Notes: 1. The student count is for Columbia College; faculty count is for Columbia University, main division.
2. In the endowed colleges, 12.2 percent of the faculty is female; 27.6 percent of the faculty in the statutory colleges is comprised of women. Internal counts by the office of the dean of the faculty show that 10 percent of the university faculty at Cornell is comprised of women.
3. Now merged with Harvard University.

Table 2. *Women* v. *Academe,* 1971–81: Fifty Cases of Interest

1971	*Green* v. *Texas Tech University*	335 F. Supp. 249 (N.D. Tex. 1971), *aff'd,* 474 F. 2d 594 (5th Cir. 1973), *reh. denied,* 475 F. 2d 1404 (5th Cir. 1973)

The plaintiff, an associate professor of english, had been teaching for almost twenty-five years at Texas Tech and had applied periodically since 1962 for promotion to full professor. She produced evidence of her professional competence and achievements and additional evidence to support allegations of a pattern of discrimination against women in her field. But the court ruled that the denial of promotion was due to her record, not her sex. The judge concluded that he should not substitute his judgment "for the rational and well-considered judgment of those possessing expertise in the field."

1972	*Abramson* v. *University of Hawaii*	56 H.A.W. 680, 548 P. 2d 253 (1976), 19 E.P.D. 9136 (9th Cir. 1979), 594 F. 2d 202

Joan Abramson was denied tenure in the English department in 1971, despite positive recommendations of the University Personnel Committee and the Faculty Senate Committee. In 1972, she filed an equal pay complaint with the Department of Labor and was terminated two weeks later. DOL secured her reinstatement with a 53 percent pay increase, but her contract was terminated the following year. When she disputed that decision, the university abolished her program. Still pending after ten years.

Braden v. *University of Pittsburgh*	343 F. Supp. 836 (W. D. Pa. 1972), 477 F. 2d 1 (3rd Cir. 1975), 13 E.P.D. 584 (3rd Cir. 1977)

A woman assistant professor alleged that the university discriminated against women in all areas of employment. In 1972, the district court found no private right of action under the exeuctive order; a higher court reversed that decision on the grounds that the university is an "instrumentality" of the state's system of higher education. In 1977, the district court declined to grant the university's motion to dismiss the case. But, before a decision could be reached on the merits of the case, plaintiff Braden died.

League of Academic Women v. *Regents of the University of California*	343 F. Supp. 636 (N.D. Cal. 1972), 4 F. E. P. Cases 808

Twelve women sued Berkeley. Of these, three were graduate students (potential employees), one was a former academic employee, and the others were either academic or nonacademic staff. They sought to represent all women employed (or qualified to be employed) for the previous five years. Academic institutions were exempt from coverage under Title VII of the Civil Rights Act until the 1972 amendments, so the plaintiffs had to bring suit under the Civil Rights Acts of 1866 and 1871. They lost.

1974

Faro v. *New York University*   502 F. 2d 1229 (2d Cir. 1974)

Ruling that the plaintiff had failed to show that she was a victim of sex discrimination, the judge ridiculed both her and her efforts: "Dr. Faro, in effect, envisions herself as a modern Jeanne d'Arc fighting for the rights of embattled womanhood on an academic battlefield, facing a solid phalanx of males and male faculty prejudice."

Gilinsky v. *Columbia*   62 F.R.D. 178 (S.D. N.Y. 1974)
University

The university claimed that a plaintiff seeking tenure could not represent a class of all academic women because her interests were, in some cases, antagonistic to theirs. The court ruled that there was no conflict among class members regarding the central issue of discrimination on the basis of sex, since presumably all class members would benefit from the elimination of such discrimination. The court, however, found in favor of the university, as did the New York Division of Human Rights.

Rackin v. *University of*   386 F. Supp. 992 (E.D. Pa. 1974)
Pennsylvania

The court ruled that a university was an instrumentality of the state and thus could be sued under the Civil Rights Act of 1866. The dispute was settled out of court with Phyllis Rackin being granted $70,000 back pay and the promotion she had been denied. Several years later, at a 1980 Cornell University conference, her colleague Robert Davies commented that another salutary outcome was that the court had subpoenaed Rackin's dossier and "the outrageous things people had said about her were made public."

Van de Vate v. *Boling*   379 F. Supp. 925 (E.D. Tenn. 1974)

The plaintiff, a woman musician, alleged that she had been denied a post at the University of Tennessee because of her sex. The judge ruled that the decision was the result of "a personality clash between the individuals involved, nothing more." The court concluded that a university's discretion "in refusing to hire an applicant because it is felt such person could not harmoniously perform his or her duties" should not be disturbed.

1975   *Cohen* v. *Illinois Institute of*   384 F. Supp. 202 (N.D. Ill.
            Technology   1974), *aff'd,* 524 F. 2d 818 (7th
            Cir. 1975), *cert. denied,* 425 U.S.
            943

Helen Cohen filed suit in 1974 after HEW said there was reasonable cause to believe that the college had discriminated against
her in denying her tenure and paying her less than similarly
situated men. The district court dismissed the case; the court of
appeals upheld that decision; the Supreme Court was asked to
review the case but did not.

McKillop v. *Regents of the*   386 F. Supp. 1270 (N.D. Cal.
University of California   1975)

This case involved a woman professor in the department of art.
The court upheld the university's insistence on the need for confidentiality in tenure decisions.

Weise v. *Syracuse University*   522 F. 2d 397

Selene Weise, an unsuccessful candidate for a lectureship, sued
on the basis of sex discrimination. The court ruled that she had
not followed proper procedures in filing with the EEOC, that the
rejection had come about before universities were bound by Title
VII, and that Syracuse, as a private university, could not be sued
for denying her constitutional rights to equal protection under the
law. The Second Circuit Court of Appeals reversed these decisions on all counts. Weise was joined in this action by Jo Davis
Mortenson, former assistant professor of English, who charged
sex discrimination in denial of tenure. In reviewing Mortenson's
case, the judge noted that she had been told, when she was
single, that she had been passed over in favor of a male because
he was married and it was a tough year to find a job. By the next
year, she was married to a colleague; then she was told that she
would not be retained because tenure could not be granted to
both a husband and a wife. Neither plaintiff has received any
satisfaction or final judgment.

1976   *Clark* v. *Atlanta University*   F.E.P. 1138 (N.D. Ga. 1976)

The judge ruled against the plaintiff, noting that he declined to
second-guess "such a subjective determination and leap to the
conclusion that racial or sexual discrimination accounts for the
perceived gap in advancement, compensation, or recognition."

Cramer v. *Virginia*   415 F. Supp. 673 (E.D. Va.
Commonwealth University   1976), 486 F. Supp. 187, 586 F.
            2d 297

Favoring a white male plaintiff claiming reverse discrimination,
the judge opined that affirmative action only perpetuates dis-

crimination. A higher court vacated this decision and remanded the case for further study because a university memorandum indicating that Cramer had been considered and found to be less qualified than the women candidate came to light. The case was dismissed.

Dyson v. Lavery   417 F. Supp. 103 (E.D. Va. 1976)

The court ruled that the plaintiff, a faculty wife, had been purposefully discriminated against "from the beginning of the interviewing process to her actual hiring" at a lower rank and salary than comparable males. She was awarded back pay. But the court also upheld Virginia Polytechnic Institute's right not to renew her appointment on the grounds that they were seeking to upgrade the institution's academic standards.

Lamphere v. Brown University 71 F. R. D. 641 (D. R. I. 1976),
                    553 F. 2d 714 (1st Cir. 1977)

Four women charged the university with sex discrimination in hiring, promotion, reappointment, and granting of tenure. After the matter had been certified as a class action, it was settled out of court. The university did not acknowledge that it had been guilty of sex discrimination, but it did agree to institute university-wide changes in procedures for recruitment, selection, and promotion, and to grant tenure to three of the plaintiffs (including anthropologist Louise Lamphere) and a cash settlement to the fourth, for whom tenure had not been at issue.

Mecklenberg v. Montana State 13 E.P.D. 11, 438, 13 F.E.P.
University   Cases 462 (D. Mont. 1976)

In this, thought to be the first successful academic class action brought by women, plaintiffs established that women faculty were clustered in the lower ranks and altogether absent from from some fields. The court took the extraordinary step of ordering the university and the plaintiffs to settle; they did. This resulted in salary adjustments for the women, awards of back pay, and a promotion for Mecklenberg.

Melani v. Board of Education 17 F. E. P. Cases 1618 (S.D. N.Y. 1976)

The judge granted class action certification to "females who are, were, or have sought to be employed as professional members of the institutional staff of various units of [the City University of New York]." The judge noted that "while it appears to be undisputed that questions of employment and promotion are made initially by individual department committees, the ultimate ratifier of these decisions and the only employer of all the members of the alleged class is the defendant Board." He noted that, even if the board only served to approve hiring, termination, and promotion decisions, pro forma, that did not excuse it from any of the legal consequences which might flow from its actions.

Pace College v. New York City   11 E.P.D. 10, 685 (N.Y.S. Ct.
Human Rights Commission   App. 1975), 394 F. Supp. 1324
(S. D. N. Y. 1975)

The commission sued on behalf of Valentine Winsey, who claimed that she was denied tenure because of her sex. The college said she was a "troublemaker"; the judge responded that "what Dr. Winsey did to cause her termination would not have been considered 'troublesome' if she had not been a woman." Winsey was awarded $75,000 in back pay and reinstatement.

Peters v. Middlebury College   409 F. Supp. 857 (D. Vt. 1976)

The plaintiff was told that she was too involved in the women's movement and too political, that is, her teaching was seen to be too feminist. The chair of her department wrote to the president of the college, explaining the decision not to reappoint as based in part on the fact that she was a "little too assertive" in her teaching. Middlebury College argued that her lack of expertise in literature was the real reason for her being denied reappointment, a defense the court accepted.

Sanday v. Carnegie Mellon   17 F.E.P. Cases 562 (W.D. Pa.
University   1976), 15 E.P.D. 8088 (W.D. Pa.
1976)

Peggy R. Sanday, denied tenure in the School of Urban and Public Affairs at Carnegie Mellon University, filed a class action, seeking to represent all women faculty at the university. The court ruled that the autonomy of the schools within the university and the departments within the schools meant that there was no "general or broad-scale policy regarding its faculty personnel which can be said to be uniformly applicable to all"—and thus, no basis for class action. Citing the *Faro* decision, the judge said: "Under such time-honored concepts as 'academic freedom' and 'merit selection,' we shall decline plaintiff's invitation to tell CMU how to run its academic affairs."

Solin v. State University of   416 F. Supp. 536 (S.D. N.Y.
New York   1976)

Plaintiff Esther Solin claimed that SUNY discriminated against Caucasian female employees and applicants. The court ruled that there was not sufficient evidence to establish the need for a class action.

1977

Cussler v. University of   430 F. Supp. 602 (D. MD. 1977)
Maryland

The issue in this case was promotion from associate to full professor, which plaintiff Cussler was denied in 1968, 1970, and 1971. Two faculty committees decided in Cussler's favor; HEW investigated and ruled for her; the Women's Equity Action League supported her case. The judge, however, ruled against her, limiting proof of discrimination to post-1972 actions and citing the *Faro* decision as a reason for deferring to academics. He commented in open court, in front of a jury, that the suit did not belong in court and that sex bias laws should perhaps not be on the books.

Johnson v. University of   435 F. Supp. 1328 (W.D. Pa.
Pittsburgh   1977), 359 F. Supp. 1002 (W.D.
     Pa. 1973)

Biochemist Sharon Johnson was denied tenure, and she sued; the district court issued an injunction against her being terminated, leading many to believe that she would win on the merits of her case. But the judge, after hearing seventy-three witnesses in a trial lasting seventy-four days, noted that this "necessitated the examination of the professional credentials of numerous professors, a task for which the court like probably most federal judges was ill suited." Elsewhere in his opinion, he stated that the court is not a "super tenure committee to pass on qualifications for and grants of tenure." The university persuaded him that their reasons for denying Johnson tenure (ineffective teaching and undertaking research irrelevant to the mission of the department) were nondiscriminatory. The judge acknowledged that she was an outstanding scientist and that she had indeed fulfilled the requirements for tenure stated to her in a letter from her department chairperson: " . . . a few publications and the concomitant election to membership by the American Society for Biological Chemists would satisfy these requirements." But that letter was unofficial, he noted, and concluded his long decision with the observation that, unless a plaintiff can prove she has been discriminated against on the basis of sex, decisions about tenure should be left "to the PhDs in academia."

Keyes v. Lenoir Rhyne College   552 F. 2d 579 (4th Cir. 1977),
     cert. denied, 434 U.S. 904

Plaintiffs offered evidence to show that, despite comparable degrees and experience, women received less pay than men and were promoted more slowly. The college advanced various reasons for individual salary differences, which the court accepted as nondiscriminatory.

| *Perham* v. *Ladd* | 16 E.P.D. 8136 (N.D. Ill. 1977), 436 F. Supp. 1101 |

Bernadette Perham, assistant professor of mathematics at Chicago State University, was denied tenure and sued, offering statistics comparing the percentage of men and women employees at CSU; an affidavit of a former professor that she was better qualified than the male promoted to tenure when she was not; and evidence of procedural failures alleged to imply a disposition to choose a man. The court held that her statistics were irrelevant because they did not indicate gross disparities and because she had failed to compare the percentage of women hired with the percentage of women in the relevant labor market but that her other evidence was sufficient to establish a prima facie case, since CSU had violated its own policy in considering a male for tenure before he had taught for seven years. The judge ruled against Perham's motion for a ruling in her favor on the grounds that she had not proven her qualification for tenure; he also ruled against the university's motion for a ruling favoring the institution on the grounds that it had not proven that the reasons for not promoting Perham were legitimate and nondiscriminatory. He did say, however, that "professional disagreements with members of an academic department are sufficient, non-discriminatory reasons to deny tenure."

| *Presseisen* v. *Swarthmore College* | 442 F. Supp. 593 (E.D. Pa. 1977), *aff'd*, 582 F. 2d 1275, 71 F.R.D. 34 (E.D. Pa. 1977) |

Plaintiff Barbara Presseisen, an assistant professor of education, charged that she had not been informed of the terminal nature of her contract, that a male fresh out of graduate school was hired to replace her at a salary a thousand dollars higher than hers had been, and that a woman candidate was turned down for the post on the grounds of being overqualified. The EEOC joined Presseisen in this class action. After months of testimony, the judge ruled for Swarthmore, saying she would have had to prove not only that there was disparate treatment of males and females but that there was intent to discriminate against females. He did establish that the existence of subjective decision-making does not defeat the argument that groups of plaintiffs have common interests and can be granted class action status.

| *Sweeney* v. *Keene State College* | 569 F. 2d 169, 176 (1st Cir. 1978), 439 U.S. 24 (1978), 48 U.S.L.W. 3465 (Jan. 21, 1981) |

Plaintiff held that her promotion had been unfairly delayed while less qualified males were promoted. Keene State said officially that her work was not mature or creative enough, but the president told Sweeney that she was rigid, narrow-minded, and inflexible. The judge ruled for Sweeney, saying that "one familiar aspect of sex discrimination is the practice, whether conscious or unconscious, of subjecting women to higher standards of evaluation than are applied to their male counterparts." The judge also reprimanded officials at Keene State for not pursuing their affirmative action program vigorously enough. Sweeney was awarded back pay and attorneys' fees in this often-cited case.

1978　　　　　*Brown* v. *Wood*　　　　　16 E.P.D. 8171

Brown, a music professor at the University of Alaska, filed a suit in 1976 claiming that the university engaged in unequal pay practices. The judge would not accept plaintiff's evidence of general university-wide pay discrepancies and accepted the university's defense that any differences in faculty salaries were based on personal evaluations and differences in experience and credentials. The Alaska Supreme Court reversed this decision, saying that the lower court should have permitted the general statistical evidence to be introduced.

Cap v. *Lehigh University*　　　433 F. Supp. 1275, 450 F. Supp. 460 (E.D. Pa. 1978)

The court ruled against plaintiff Cap, an assistant professor of French, on the grounds that the male to whom she compared herself was more qualified for promotion to tenure than she. One of the arguments she advanced was that her department head, a woman, reportedly believed that Cap should have stayed at home with her child rather than continuing to work at the university.

EEOC v. *Tufts Institution of Learning*　　　421 F. Supp. 152, 157 (D. Mass. 1975)

The Equal Employment Opportunity Commission sued on behalf of two women who had not been awarded tenure, asking the court to issue an injunction against their termination. The commission argued that their department chair was acknowledged to have "an Old World concept of woman's place in the university." The judge ruled that one of the two was affected more than the other by his attitudes; she was granted injunctive relief.

Hill v. *Nettleton*　　　22 E.P.D. 30,810 (D. Col. 1978), 455 F. Supp. 514

The court ruled in favor of the plaintiff, an instructor-coach-administrator in the women's athletic program at Colorado State University who had campaigned vigorously for equal opportunities for women within the institution. The judge said, "Not only was the plaintiff treated less favorably than other faculty members because of her position as a symbol of sexual equality, she was also a victim of a system which has a disparate impact on females." The plaintiff won $65,000 in damages.

Kunda v. *Muhlenberg College*   22 F.E.P. Cases 62 (3rd Cir.
                                   1980), 621 F. 2d 532 (3rd Cir.
                                   1980), 22 E.P.D. 30,674

The plaintiff was not awarded tenure, allegedly because she
lacked a master's degree. In her trial, she demonstrated that some
men had been promoted without terminal degrees, that the faculty handbook described the requirement as a terminal degree or
its equivalent, and that she had had the strong support of her
review committee. Thus, she was not challenging the validity of
peer review. The court ordered Muhlenberg to offer the plaintiff
tenure when she obtained her master's degree, which she did and
it did.

Powell v. *Syracuse University*   580 F. 2d 1150, 1154 (2d Cir.
                                     1978), 439 U.S. 984 (1978)

Citing the deferential standard of the *Faro* decision, the court
ruled against plaintiff Powell, who claimed sex discrimination in a
negative tenure decision. The circuit court reviewed the decision,
upholding it, but opined that this should not be interpreted to
mean that a court could never intervene in an academic institution's personnel decisions, as the first judge had implied.

Smith College v.   18 E.P.D. 8699 (Mass Sup. Ct.
Massachusetts Commission   1978), 38 N.E. 2d 121
against Discrimination

Maurianne Adams and Mary Carruther, assistant professors of
English, filed with the MCAD, alleging sex discrimination in denial of tenure. The commission ordered reinstatement with tenure
and back pay. Smith College appealed this decision, and the
judge ruled against the women, saying that the MCAD had failed
to recognize that proof of discriminatory motive is critical.

Townsel v. *University of*   80 F.R.D. 741 (N.D. Ala. 1978)
Alabama

The court stated that "equal employment opportunity suits involving academic positions at colleges or universities are ill suited
for class actions because the decisions in question must be individually scrutinized."

1979   *Cooper* v. *University of Texas*   482 F. Supp. 187 (N.D. Tex.
                at Dallas   1979), *aff'd,* 648 F. 2d 1039

The court established that a plaintiff complaining of discrimination in hiring could represent class members complaining of tenure practices. But plaintiff Mary Weiss Cooper lost. The dean
claimed that, in 1973, when he hired a male candidate to teach
operations research, he thought there would be two posts and he

planned to offer the second to Dr. Cooper. But there was an
unexpected budget cut. In 1975, when the university could hire a
second person in the field, it chose a male candidate who had
guided thirteen doctoral students, while Dr. Cooper's Ph.D. thesis was not sure to be published and she had written only one
other article. These were accepted by the court as legitimate, nondiscriminatory reasons for not hiring Cooper.

1979

Eichman v. Indiana State   597 F.2d 1104 (1979), 19 E.P.D.
University Board of Trustees   9179 (7th Cir. 1979)

Plaintiff Thomas Lee Eichman was not reappointed as assistant
professor of German. He filed suit, claiming that his constitutional rights to free speech, liberty, property, equal protection,
and substantive and procedural due process had been violated by
this decision and also that it was in relatiation for his having
assisted a woman colleague to assert her Title VII rights. The
district court ruled against him on all counts, but the Seventh
Circuit Court of Appeals reversed in part, saying that his right to
free speech might have been compromised because he had criticized his employer. Further, the court ruled that he was protected
from retaliation under Title VII because he had in fact assisted a
woman colleague to file a grievance with the EEOC, alleging sex
discrimination. He and two other faculty men were specifically
mentioned as supporting the grievant in the EEOC complaint;
none of the three was reappointed the following year.

Fisher v. Flynn   598 F. 2d 663 (1st Cir. 1979), 19
                         E.P.D. 9204, 9209

An assistant professor at Bridgewater State College charged that
her department chairperson had sexually harassed her. The court
ruled that "plaintiff has not alleged a sufficient nexus between her
refusal to accede to the romantic overtures and her termination.
She has not alleged that the department chairman had the authority to terminate her employment or effectively recommend the
same and we cannot so assume." The court declined to rule on
the issue of whether or not sexual harassment could constitute a
violation of Title VII.

Molthan v. Temple University 83 F.R.D. 368 (E.D. Pa. 1979),
                                442 F. Supp. 448

A woman physician sued because she had been demoted to a
non-tenure-track position, allegedly because she took a consulting
job that took four hours a month. Another plaintiff, in sociology
and education, complained that a new department chair had
hired a new male to teach her courses. The court ruled that a class
of aggrieved plaintiffs could meet the requirement of "commonal-
ity" and thus be certified as a class, even though no single specified allegedly discriminatory policy which affected everybody in

the class had been identified. The judge, however, ruled that Molthan's job was unique, thus she could not claim the protection of the Equal Pay Act.

1980   *Blaubergs* v. *University of*   625 F. 2d 1146
           Georgia

Judge Wilbur Owens asked James Dinnan how he had voted on the tenure candidacy of the plaintiff, former women's studies director Maija Blaubergs. Dinnan refused to respond, claiming his academic freedom was being violated; the judge sentenced him to serve three months in jail, which he did.

Campbell v. *Ramsey*   484 F. Supp. 190 (E.D. Ark. 1980), *aff'd*, 631 F. 2d 597

The issue here was reappointment. Plaintiff Caroline Campbell, a mathematician, charged the University of Arkansas at Little Rock with sex discrimination when she was terminated because she did not have an advanced degree. The university acknowledged that it was "not necessary" for her particular position, but persuaded the court that upgrading the faculty was a legitimate, nondiscriminatory reason for terminating Campbell. She argued that this seemingly neutral practice had disparate effects on men and women; the university rebutted this successfully by showing that it was justified by the business necessity of upgrading the department.

Jepsen v. *Florida Board of*   22 E.P.D. 30, 624 (1980), 610 F.
Regents   2d 1379 (5th Cir. 1980)

Laura Jepsen, an associate professor for twenty-five years, claimed that males with comparable qualifications were promoted in five to six years. The first court, in a two day trial, dismissed her case, saying judges should be reluctant to intervene in academic decision making. The higher court remanded and reversed the decision, ruling that the university must divulge confidential evaluations of other professors to plaintiffs and that a court should admit such evidence when an institution relies on them to counter discrimination claims. The judge opined that "caution against intervention in a university's affairs cannot be allowed to undercut the explicit legislative intent of Title VII. . . ."

Lieberman v. *Gant*   630 F. 2d 60 (2d Cir. 1980), 23 E.P.D. 31, 164

The judge ruled against plaintiff Marcia Lieberman, who claimed that the negative tenure decision at the University of Connecticut was due to the fact that she is a woman and a strong advocate of women's rights, and for Gant, representing the trustees, administrators, and faculty at UC. The judge had reviewed some ten thousand pages of transcript and four hundred exhibits. He concluded that the nature of tenure, which entails "what is close to a life-long commitment by a university," affords institutions discretion. A decision about tenure is, he ruled, subjective.

Manning v. *Trustees of Tufts College*   22 E.P.D. 30,620 (1st Cir. 1980)

Diane Manning alleged that she had been denied tenure on the basis of her sex and asked the court to grant an injunction against her termination. The judge ruled that she had not shown probability of success on the merits of her case. She then filed a motion to vacate on the grounds that Tufts had withheld documents that she needed to prepare her case. The court ruled there was no malice in that action. Another issue in this complicated case was the fact that she had not received authorization to sue from the EEOC; the court did not rule on this problem.

Marshall v. *Georgia Southwestern College*   24 E.P.D. 17,867 (1980), 489 F. Supp. 1322

The same court that sent James Dinnan to jail ruled that Georgia Southwestern had discriminated against six women faculty members. Responding to the college's defense that salary disparities were due to differences in merit and differences in supply and demand for specialists in different fields, Judge Owens ruled that "mentally and physically the effort required of all teaching faculty members is substantially the same."

Rajender v. *University of Minnesota*   20 E.P.D. 30, 225 (D. Minn. 1979), 24 F.E.P. Cases 1045 (D. Minn. 1978)

The plaintiff was denied a tenure-track post in chemistry in 1973 and filed a suit that was certified as a class action. The court awarded her $100,000, imposed a quota for the hiring of women in chemistry, and appointed a special master to resolve all past or future sex discrimination grievances at the university. The master is empowered to award cash damages and faculty positions, including tenured posts, and to oversee hiring there until 1989.

1981   *Carton* v. *Trustees of Tufts College*   E.P.D. 31,630, 25 F.E.P. Cases 1114 (D. Mass. 1981)

In the course of its deliberations, the court scrutinized the intent of the plaintiff's departmental colleagues, the members of her ad hoc committee, the six faculty members of her tenure and promotion committee, the dean, the provost, and the president of the college. The judge ultimately ruled against Lonnie Carton, concluding that "the determinative factor in the negative decision was [plaintiff's] lack of traditional scholarship."

Lynn v. Regents of the	21 E.P.D. 30, 58 (1979), 27
University of California	E.P.D. 32, 149

Therese Lynn, a specialist on the influence of women on the development of French literature, was denied tenure and sued, claiming sex discrimination. The district court dismissed her charge, saying that the university had articulated legitimate and nondiscriminatory reasons for the decision. The court of appeals ruled, however, that Lynn had in fact established a prima facie case of sex discrimination and that the university had withheld documents from her that were pertinent to the case. Perhaps most significantly, the judge stated: "A disdain for women's issues, and a diminished opinion of those who concentrate on those issues, is evidence of a discriminatory attitude towards women."

Michigan State University	Slip opinion No. G–76–649 C.A.
Faculty Association v.	5 (W.D. Mich., Oct. 13, 1981)
Michigan State University	

Five women faculty members claimed sex discrimination in employment at Michigan State; the judge certified them as representing a class composed of female faculty. But in October 1981, Judge Benjamin Gibson withdrew the class certification on the grounds that the disputed decisions were made in individual, autonomous departments and not by the university as a whole. The judge noted that he could not certify women in each department as a class because "there is insufficient evidence of the requisite numerosity in such an approach." Thus, there was no class action in the Michigan State case because the university is too big and diverse but the departments within it are too small, with too few women.

Penk v. Oregon State Board of	Slip opinion C. 80–436 (D.
Education	Oreg., October 13, 1981)

Judge Helen Frye certified as a class action a suit brought by thirteen women faculty members from Oregon campuses. The named plaintiffs could represent as many as fifteen hundred current and former women faculty.

Bibliography

1. *AAUP Policy Documents and Reports.* Washington, D.C.: American Association of University Professors, 1977.

This ninety-eight-page booklet contains statements of AAUP policies affecting academic freedom, tenure, and due process; college and university government; collective bargaining; professional ethics; student rights and freedoms; college and university accreditation; research and teaching; collateral benefits; and the constitution of the association. Of particular interest are the sections dealing with antinepotism rules; leaves for childbearing, child rearing, and family emergencies; and recommended institutional regulations on academic freedom and tenure. The latter regulations call for written terms of appointment; provision of information to candidates on standards for appointment renewal, procedures by which that decision will be made, and timing of decisions regarding nonrenewal; and similar forms of notification. Not all institutions subscribe to these regulations or adhere to them even in spirit. Some academics in nonsubscribing institutions lament that fact. Others have less enthusiasm for AAUP policies, especially one regarding procedures for grieving a negative tenure decision, which stipulates that the review committee will not substitute its judgment on the merits of decisions for that of the faculty body, i.e., reviewing committees will confine themselves to a consideration of whether or not appropriate procedures were followed.

2. Abramson, Joan. *The Invisible Woman: Discrimination in the Academic Profession.* San Francisco: Jossey-Bass, 1975.

This book details, step by step, the process by which the author tried to appeal a negative tenure decision announced to her in December 1970 by the University of Hawaii. She suspected that her status as faculty wife had affected the committee's decision. This was never more evident than when she met with the president of the university to ask that he investigate her charge of sex discrimination by the English department: She was permitted to have her husband present as her "advisor on university administrative practices," and several weeks later, the

president wrote a memorandum confirming the agreement reached at
the meeting to her husband. The author responded by writing to the
president's wife, asking her to advise her husband that his memorandum had been received. Abramson devotes the first section of her book
to her own case, which culminated in her being fired in September
1973. Other sections deal systematically with her efforts to find help
from the AAUP (an organization she deems the "Status Quo Seekers");
the U.S. Department of Labor (slow and ineffective); HEW (slower and
less effective); the EEOC (the "Paper Tiger"); and the ultimate disap-
pointment, the courts. Her advice to academic administrators is solid.
Her counsel to grievants: hang on. To all readers: academic women
mean business.

3. ———. *Old Boys, New Women: The Politics of Sex Discrimination.* New
York: Praeger, 1979.

This solidly researched book is devoted to sex discrimination grievances
filed against academic institutions and other employers of professionals. There are quotations from hundreds of court decisions (most of
them ruling against the grievants) and reports from the few women
who have won but have found their victories hollow (for example, one
of the plaintiffs in the *Mecklenburg* v. *Montana State* case). Some of the
evidence is disillusioning, for example, supposedly neutral requests
from department chairpersons asking for outside opinions. When the
department chair at the University of Pittsburgh wrote for outside advice on the promotion of Sharon Johnson, the letter writer prefaced his
remarks by saying that the department had already decided her work
was not good enough. Jenijoy LaBell's case at the California Institute of
Technology is also instructive. LaBell was denied tenure because it was
said that she failed to measure up to the newly instituted "Princeton
standard," that is, she had not had a manuscript accepted by a press of
the stature of Princeton's. A matter of days later, she got word that her
book had been accepted by none other than Princeton University Press.
But she was still not promoted; the standards, it appeared, had
changed again. Abramson has harsh criticism for the ineptitude and
foot-dragging of the enforcement agencies. Given all the problems, why
do women file suits? "They have become justifiably angered at the
system and they have decided that there are times when fighting injustice is better than silent suffering, even when one grasps the fact that
the world is not always just."

4. **"Academic Freedom and Federal Regulation of University Hiring."** *Harvard Law Review* 92, 4 (February 1979): 879–97.

The question considered in this article is whether or not there are constitutional claims that may be asserted by colleges and universities to

resist government regulation of their hiring and promotion policies. The article concludes that while the autonomy of educational institutions appears to merit constitutional protection, "the present government policy of funding only those institutions which comply with federal hiring regulations appears constitutional."

5. *Affirmative Action in Employment in Higher Education: A Consultation Sponsored by the U.S. Commission on Civil Rights.* Washington, D.C.: U. S. Commission on Civil Rights, 1975.

This conference was a forum in which there was little agreement. Charles V. Willie, a black professor formerly at Syracuse University, recounted his personal experiences with racism; an economist, Thomas Sowell, then professor of economics, UCLA, presented extensive data to support his view that affirmative action was not needed in higher education; and activist Bernice Sandler declared that it would be tragic if affirmative action were abandoned. "Affirmative action is coming under a good deal or criticism, partly because it has been badly administered and partly because some administrators have misunderstood the Federal requirements," Sandler said. "If women and minorities are to have the birthright that is that of their white brothers, they must have the opportunity to partake in the fruits of higher education as students, as staff, as faculty, as administrators. To weaken *any* of the laws that protect them from discrimination . . . [would be] a denial of the rights of women and minorities."

6. **Ahern, Nancy C., and Scott, Elizabeth L.** *Career Outcomes in a Matched Sample of Men and Women Ph.D.s: An Analytical Report* (Washington, D.C.: Committee on the Education and Employment of Women in Science and Engineering, Commission on Human Resources, National Research Council, National Academy Press, 1981)

This careful study compares the career histories of 15,492 women and men who earned the Ph.D. in mathematics, natural sciences, social and behavioral sciences, and the humanities between 1940 and 1979. As Lilli S. Hornig, chair of the committee that sponsored the study, notes in the introduction, sex differences in salary and rank "might arise for many reasons unrelated to discrimination—among them, for example, women's presumed larger investment of time and energy in marriage and parenting, and their presumed restricted geographic mobility. . . ." Well-matched samples of men and women holders of doctorates were analyzed. The results suggest strongly that the differences in status are not due to the commonly accepted explanations but to the fact that men discriminate against women. Hornig notes that the disparities vary by academic discipline; this "suggests forcefully that the disadvantages women suffer have little to do with marriage, family responsibilities, or limited geographic mobility." Among the favorable reviews of this study was one by Colin Norman in the November 20, 1981, issue of *Science* ("Sex Discrimination Persists in Academe"), who lauded it for "exploding some of the myths about why sex differences in academic rank and pay occur."

7. **Aiken, Ray J. "Legal Liabilities in Higher Education: Their Scope and Management."** *Journal of College and University Law* 3; 2, 3, 4 (1976): 7–214.

The premise on which this lengthy article is based is that educational institutions should be assisted to minimize their risks, which are, because of the nature of the enterprise and the law governing it, substantial. The author, who is both university legal counsel and a professor of law, begins by describing a typical case, *Weise* v. *Syracuse University*, and summarizes an argument that appears in many cases: if women are underrepresented in an academic institution, can we assume this is because of discrimination? Will any other reasons advanced by the institution be dismissed as pretexts, sham, or unconvincing? He notes elsewhere that "there may be some concern whether either the claimants or the defendants will live to see the final vindication of one or the other position." Many academic cases are cited; the overall theme is that attorneys should assist their institutions to ensure that the courts will still keep hands off personnel practices in faculty recruitment, selection, and promotion. Citing *Mecklenburg* v. *Montana State University* as a fundamentally bad decision, the author states that the court translated goal-oriented stipulations from the institution's affirmative action plan into evidence of "tortious discrimination" on the part of the university.

8. **Astin, Helen.** *The Woman Doctorate in America: Origins, Career, and Family.* New York: Russell Sage Foundation, 1969.

One thousand six hundred fifty-three women who earned the Ph.D. at American institutions during 1957 and 1958 were surveyed in January 1966. Was the investment in their education wasted? Not at all. Ninety-one percent were working, 81 percent full time. Their achievement was high. The problems they encountered were lack of household help, negative attitudes of their husbands, and to some extent, their husbands' occupational mobility. The second most formidable group of problems reported involved employer discrimination. The women who were professionally active, had published a great deal, and had been recognized for professional achievement were the most likely to report employer discrimination.

9. **Baldwin, Stephen E.** " 'Subconscious' Sex Bias and Labor Market Reality." *Labor Law Journal* 30, 7 (July 1979): 439–40.

Are women taking jobs away from men? Hardly, says economist Baldwin. To rationalize men's resentment of women workers on that basis is to ignore reality, he says. Responding to the suggestion in an article by J. H. Foegen (1979) that another reason men resent working women is that they are bitter about two-paycheck families, Baldwin points out that two-job families are here to stay, whether breadwinners from one-paycheck families like it or not. Furthermore, there are four million families where there is only one earner: a woman. The problem, he concludes, is not the resentment anybody may feel. It is the discrimination that women and blacks experience in the labor market.

10. **Berger, Margaret A.** *Litigation on Behalf of Women: A Review for the Ford Foundation.* New York: Ford Foundation, 1980.

This is a review of the extent to which recent cases have improved the status of women with regard to a wide variety of issues: pension plans, pregnancy, disparate impact of facially neutral policies, and so forth. It is surprising to read how many cases have been funded by the Ford Foundation. Grantees of the Ford Foundation and others interviewed for this report lament that judges "do not respond to claims of sex discrimination with the same feeling of urgency with which they react to racial discrimination." Drawing from various court decisions, this author notes that judges are hostile to women plaintiffs who claim sex discrimination in academic life, characterizing them as "pushy, over-sensitive, troublemakers" and ridiculing them for viewing themselves as modern Joans of Arc. Berger calls for more effective strategies to locate plaintiffs with strong cases and more careful choices of jurisdiction to yield better results in academic discrimination cases.

11. **Bernard, Jessie.** *Academic Women.* University Park, Pa.: Pennsylvania State University Press, 1964.

In this pioneering work, Bernard reported on the results of new studies and drew together findings of earlier work. Her tables show that academic women differ from their male counterparts in several important characteristics: marital status (women more likely to remain single, or if married, to be divorced); IQ as measured by IQ tests (women higher); and productivity (men higher). On the issue of productivity, she notes that women are employed by different kinds of institutions than men, and the kind of institution is a better predictor of productivity than sex is. She quotes generously from women professors' comments on their own satisfactions and problems. In an appendix, she cites a study done at Pennsylvania State that suggests that, when a man and a woman judged to be equally effective communicators transmit material to students, the students who hear it from the man tend to be more likely to believe it.

12. **Bogart, Karen.** *Institutional Self-Study Guide on Sex Equity for Postsecondary Educational Institutions.* Washington, D.C.: American Institutes for Research, 1981.

Organized in five booklets, this guide consists of checklists of questions designed to help identify policies and practices that may affect sex equity for students, faculty, administrators, and staff. The guide was developed and field-tested with grants from the Carnegie Corporation of New York. It is based on a study of perceptions of discrimination, which involved interviews with more than two hundred administrators, faculty members, students, researchers, plaintiffs, attorneys, and others. The questions and the responses to them suggest possible actions to detect, prevent, and remedy sex inequities. Sample questions to faculty: Does each department have explicit criteria for promotion to tenure? Are these criteria transmitted to each candidate? If a decision is appealed, is there provision for the review to be conducted by faculty other than those who made the original decision? Sample questions for all concerned faculty and administrators have to do with mechanisms for eliminating the subtle forms of discrimination, which, while they may take the form of nonactionable behavior, still have the effect of diminishing the quality of the educational experience of students and the quality of work life for staff and faculty. Examples given include instances of condescension on the part of faculty to women students, staff, and faculty; reports of sexist comments, jokes, and assumptions about women's ability; and practices that result in the exclusion of women from the informal professional networks.

13. **Bolarsky, Carolyn.** "Tenure in Academe: Secret Ballots and Civil Rights." *Spokeswoman* 10, 12 (December 1980): 8–9.

This article discusses the case of the University of Georgia professor, James Dinnan, who went to jail rather than reveal his vote on a woman's candidacy for tenure. Should a faculty member's right to maintain a secret ballot supersede a plaintiff's civil rights? This author says it should not. One problem with the controversy over secrecy, she notes, is that it is drawing attention away from the central issue. Ellen Mattingly, president of the Georgia chapter of the AAUP, believes that the university administration and the regents are trying to obscure the "real issues of sex and race discrimination with their open support" of Dinnan. Mattingly, an associate professor of geology, has joined with other women faculty to file a motion to amend Blaubergs's suit to be a class action. Blaubergs, having lost her faculty post, is going to law school. According to the author of this article, "Blauberg's chances of winning the case eventually appear good."

14. **Boring, Phyllis Zatlin. "Filing a Faculty Grievance."** Mimeographed. Women's Equity Action League, 805 15th St. NW, Washington, D.C. 20005, 1978.

Addressed to the grievant, or potential grievant, this straightforward article was written in June 1978 by Boring, an associate dean at Rutgers University, for her faculty colleagues. There are five succinct sections— "Evaluate Your Case," "Plan Ahead," "Learn Your Time Limits," "Consider the Psychological Toll," "Proceed with Caution"—and sound counsel. Sample observation: "Gradually, as the grievance process stretches into weeks and months, you may even develop a kind of paranoia. . . . It is common for complainants to begin to suspect the motives of even those people who have kindly volunteered their time and expertise to serve as counselors in the grievance process."

15. **Broad, William J. "Ending Sex Discrimination in Academia."** *Science* 208, 6 (June 1980): 1120–22.

Broad presents a definitive summary of one of the few cases that academic women have won, the class action suit brought by Shyamala Rajender against the University of Minnesota. Rajender was a researcher in the department of chemistry who was denied a tenure-track job. According to the author, this case set two precedents: the cash settlement is one of the highest of its kind, and, for the first time, the court established hiring quotas and the appointment of a "special master" to oversee all past or future sex discrimination claims until 1989. Rajender now practices law in San Francisco. Of the seven-year fight, she says, "At least I've done something for women in chemistry and maybe through all the university."

16. **Bunzel, John H. "The Case of the Jailed Georgia Professor: Let's Cut through the Intellectual Smog."** *Chronicle of Higher Education* 21, 18 (January 12, 1981): 96.

The author, former president of San Jose State University, argues for confidentiality in faculty review of tenure candidates and the secret ballot, which "permits a vote to be cast free of pressure from other faculty members, administrators, students, or off-campus community groups." Bunzel holds that James Dinnan should not have been ordered by U. S. district court judge Wilbur Owens to reveal how he had voted on the candidacy of Maija S. Blaubergs, former director of the University of Georgia's women's studies program. A committee set up in February 1980 reviewed the original decision to turn down Blaubergs and concluded that she had "failed to meet the required standards for promotion." And that, Bunzel implies, should have been that.

17. **Burton, Doris-Jean. "Ten Years of Affirmative Action and the Changing Status of Women in Political Science."** *PS* (American Political Science Association) 12, 1 (Winter 1979): 18–22.

Between 1969 and 1979, women's share of the academic political science positions grew from 9.1 to 10.0 percent. As in other fields, women are concentrated at the bottom ranks; the greatest gains in women's appointments were in temporary and part-time appointments, made in the last half of the decade. There still appears to be a male-female pay gap, even at the instructor level, a sign that this author terms "ominous." Overall, she notes, women have been gaining ground in the discipline, "but it is an upstream swim in a dwindling river." This article includes a useful table on the number of women and men faculty in political science in twenty distinguished institutions, by year, from 1973–74 through 1977–78. For example: Berkeley went from forty-one men and one woman in 1973 to thirty-eight men and two women in 1978; Cornell, from twenty-five men, no women to twenty-seven men, three women; Harvard, from thirty-seven men, four women to thirty-three men, two women. The author comments on the questions the numbers cannot answer: Do women prefer part-time positions? Are the two women listed on the faculty at a given institution one year the same two who were there the previous year? Are they being promoted and tenured at the same rate as men?

18. **Caplow, Theodore, and McGee, Reece J.** *The Academic Marketplace.* New York: Anchor Books, Doubleday, 1965.

Originally published in 1958, this intriguing book gives an inside view of the groves of academe resulting from a study of ten major universities in the mid-1950s. Of interest now is the careful picture of the old-boy network and the importance of recruiting colleagues who will add to the prestige of a department rather than detract from it: "Women tend to be discriminated against in the academic profession, not because they have low prestige but because they are outside the prestige system entirely and for this reason are of no use to a department in future recruitment." Discrimination on the basis of race is everywhere, the authors note, and "women scholars are not taken seriously and cannot look forward to a normal professional career." This kind of candor is refreshing today, more than thirty years later, when many other male scholars are stoutly insisting that there is no discrimination except in the minds of disgruntled women who didn't get hired or didn't get tenure. When Caplow and McGee made their observations, the behavior they described was not against the law.

19. **Carnegie Council on Policy Studies in Higher Education.** *Making Affirmative Action Work in Higher Education: An Analysis of Institutional and Federal Policies with Recommendations.* San Francisco: Jossey-Bass, 1975.

This comprehensive sourcebook for the academic administrator includes extensive suggestions for framing an affirmative action plan and implementing it. It provides a detailed review of academic policies and the ways in which they can be changed. There are chapters on goals and timetables, some rather cogent comments on the deficiencies in the administration of federal policy, pages of useful statistics, and in an appendix, examples of correspondence between universities and the government agencies.

20. **Centra, John A.** "Women, Marriage, and the Doctorate." *Findings: A Quarterly of Educational Testing Service Research in Postsecondary Education* 2, 4 (1975): 1–2.

The author reports on a survey of 3,658 persons who earned Ph.D. or Ed.D. degrees in 1950, 1960, or 1968, of whom half were women. The doctors differed by marital status: nine-tenths of the men were or had been married, as compared with two-thirds of the women. This trend was, however, changing. In 1968 more women Ph.D.'s married than did those earning their degrees earlier. The women had more career interruptions than the men; at the time of the study, more than nine-tenths of the men had worked full-time continuously since earning their degrees, as compared to about two-thirds of the women. His data showed that men published more than women. Single men and women averaged ten publications each, while married men averaged eighteen and married women nine.

21. **Churgin, Jonah R.** *The New Woman and the Old Academe: Sexism and Higher Education.* Roslyn Heights, N.Y.: Libra Publishers, 1978.

In this book, Churgin analyzes the academy and the way it affects and reflects social attitudes toward and prejudices against women. He comments that it seems the most effective way to set up a women's studies program is to have the faculty hold joint appointments, with half-time being in a traditional department and half-time being devoted to the program. In discussing affirmative action, he remarks that one way to approach it is to require faculty members to use as much ingenuity in getting minorities into the system as has been exercised over the years in keeping them out. What will be the effects of affirmative action? The author believes that departmental power will be weakened, scholars will become more interdisciplinary because they know they may be evaluated by nonspecialists, and higher education will become more meritocratic.

22. **Clark, Donald L. "Discrimination Suits: A Unique Settlement."** *Educational Record* 58, 3 (Summer 1977): 233–49.

The resolution of the Montana State University class action suit was unique, according to the author, because in 1976, federal judge W. D. Murray not only ruled in favor of the five women faculty members who claimed sex discrimination in pay and promotion, as well as underrepresentation of women as a class, but he then took unprecedented action in ordering a negotiated settlement. The author, who represented the university in the negotiations, gives a detailed description on how he and the two opposing lawyers worked out an agreement satisfactory to all parties. The master plan called for mandated representation of women on search committees and immediate addition of women to key committees dealing with promotion, tenure, and administrative decision making. Further, it set up a special review committee that could recommend promotion for women, including promotion that would be retroactive for as many as three years, and committed the administration to fund a "pairing" study to compare women's salaries with men's and consider three to four years' retroactive pay for women. The process by which this committee decided to give back pay to women faculty is detailed.

23. **Clark, Linda. "Fact and Fantasy: A Recent Profile of Women in Academia."** *Peabody Journal of Education* 54 (January 1977): 103–9.

Women were still in trouble in academe in the mid-1970s despite some progress, this author suggests. She buttresses her argument with data on underrepresentation and a review of the obstacles that seem to stand in women's way. She intersperses her data with questions addressed to educators reading the article, which she hopes will assist readers to recognize their own sex bias.

24. **Clinton, Catherine. "Women's Graves of Academe."** *New York Times*, November 5, 1980, p. A31.

The author comments on recent progress made by academic women in the courts: "The news stories tell of their triumphs in the courts—as if the pathway to fair treatment is always paved with litigation." She cites statistics to show the underrepresentation of women on the faculty at

Harvard, University of Pennsylvania, and Princeton. When universities are unabashedly hostile to women academics, she asks, "what's a female faculty member to do, but sue?"

25. **Coffinberger, Richard L., and Matthews, Frank L. "Promoting Affirmative Action through Part-Time Faculty: The Need for a Rational Policy."** *Labor Law Journal* 31, 12 (December 1980): 772–78.

The authors observe that the use of part-time faculty members is on the increase in the United States. Although they find it difficult to define part time, they note that those who teach less than full time have lower job security, higher turnover, and lower salaries—thus, their employment represents a savings to the institution. Although the executive orders are silent on the need for affirmative action among part-time faculty, the authors believe that this provides a good opportunity for administrators to go beyond the requirements of the law and actively encourage women and minority applicants for part-time, as well as full-time, positions. This would provide for a more diverse faculty and more diverse role models for students. They provide a model plan calling for affirmative advertising and recruitment and proposing that an institution be given pro rata credit, for up to 25 percent of its hiring goal for full-time faculty, for women and minorities hired as part-time faculty. The idea of extending affirmative action to part-time faculty has merit, but according to numerous other observers, women are already overrepresented among part-time, non-tenure-track faculty members at many institutions.

26. **Cole, Jonathan R.** *Fair Science: Women in the Scientific Community.* New York: Free Press, 1979.

According to Cole, a sociologist, "The measurable amount of sex-based discrimination against women scientists is small. The data do not require that we modify prior conclusions that the scientific stratification system is basically universalistic." Karen Oppenheim Mason, of the Center for Advanced Study in the Behavioral Sciences, Stanford, reviewed this book in *Science* (April 18, 1980, pp. 277–78) and found the data did not support the author's conclusion.

27. ———. **"Women in Science."** *Scientific American*, July-August, 1981: 385–91.

Cole, in an about-face, summarizes his empirical studies by saying that there is "significant gender-based discrimination in the promotion of female scientists to tenure and high academic rank." Although women scientists have as high intelligence quotients as their male colleagues do, the women publish less than the men. One reason for this, Cole says, may be that "many women continue to be excluded from the very activities that allow for full participation and growth, or productivity . . . the informal activities of science—the heated discussion and debates in the laboratory, inclusion in the inner core or the invisible colleges, full participation in the social networks where scientists air ideas and generate new ones."

28. **A Commitment to Equality: One Century Later.** Report of the Ad Hoc Trustee Committee on the Status of Women at Cornell University. Revised, as accepted by the board of trustees, March 16, 1974.

Early in 1972, the members of the board of trustees of Cornell University resolved to appoint a committee "to study the status of women students, faculty members, and employees at Cornell University and to make appropriate recommendations concerning that status." The committee gathered statistics on the number of women students by unit, the number of women faculty by rank and department (including a comparison of the faculty-student ratio by sex—1 male faculty member for every 11 male students; 1 female faculty member for every 46 female students), and data on athletic budgets (by sex) and staff appointments (by sex and race). The committee noted that it had trouble gathering the data, because some faculty members were opposed to collecting or maintaining such records, and that there were problems reconciling figures gathered from different sources. Nevertheless, the committee came up with seventeen recommendations, concluding with the important one: annual reports on progress toward resolving the problems uncovered should be made for at least five years.

29. **Conable, Charlotte Williams. "Advancing by Degrees."** *Cornell Alumni News* 80, 9 (May 1978): 3.

Focusing on opportunities for graduate education for women at Cornell, Conable relates that the first woman to earn a Cornell doctorate, May Preston, Ph.D. 1880, reported that she had to do more work than was required of the men. Fifteen years later, Cornell awarded the first doctor of science degree conferred on a woman in the United States. In 1978, Conable writes, women graduate students comprised 26 percent of the total graduate enrollment and were earning 14 percent of the doctorates awarded.

30. ———. **"The Uneven Progress of Women at Cornell."** *Human Ecology Forum* 11, 1 (Summer 1980): 16–18.

By 1980, Conable writes, women comprised 40 percent of the student body at Cornell and fully 48 percent of the graduate students in veterinary medicine. But opposition to women on the faculty was fading more slowly, so slowly that, in 1979, the university received the National Organization for Women's Silver Snail Award for "spectacularly sluggish affirmative action"—to call attention to "snail-paced enforcement of federal laws barring sex discrimination in education." In 1971, the faculty was 92.4 percent male and by 1979, 91.7 percent male.

31. ———. *Women at Cornell: The Myth of Equal Education.* Ithaca, N.Y.: Cornell University Press, 1977.

In 1870 there were only eight hundred women studying at coeducational institutions in the United States. One, Jennie Spencer of Cortland, New York, was the first woman to be admitted to Cornell University. Conable traces the history of women students at an institution where, despite the founders' insistence on the importance of equal admissions, they were not welcome. The number of women admitted over the years was restricted to the number of beds available for them in the women's dormitories, which meant that women were confined, by and large, to "womanly" areas of study. Conable traces the history of women students and faculty through 1977, by which time there was a women's studies program, the first or second in the country; a woman vice president, Constance E. Cook, '41; and no quotas on female admissions to the undergraduate and graduate schools and colleges. The first woman teacher elevated to the professorial ranks at Cornell was botanist Anna Botsford Comstock, who was appointed assistant professor in the summer session in 1898. The trustees decided it was not a suitable title for a woman and demoted her to lecturer, in which position she remained for thirteen years before finally being reappointed assistant professor in 1911 and promoted to full professor in 1920, just before her retirement.

32. Connolly, Walter B., Jr., and Peterson, David W., *Use of Statistics in Equal Employment Opportunity Litigation.* New York: Law Journal Seminars-Press, 1980.

A guide to equal employment opportunity measurement, this is an introduction to ways of ascertaining whether or not illegal discrimination has taken place. The authors summarize their method: "We have at hand some data, a history of some aspect of an employer's performance over a period of time; we construct an hypothesis or model as to how these data would be if the employer's practices over this period of time were equitable; and then we compare the observed data to the model values and determine whether the observed differences are small enough to reasonably be due to innocent chance, or whether they are so large as to indicate that reality and the model are rather different." The book is intended to help employers respond to plaintiffs' statistical presentations. Since defendants may rely on this text rather heavily, it would appear to be "must" reading for plaintiffs. Besides guiding the reader through the technicalities of computing availability of women and minorities, the authors raise some provocative questions. For example, if an employer bows to the market pressure to pay black engineers more than white engineers, since the former are in greater demand due to their scarcity, can the employer legitimately distinguish between two other kinds of labor markets: the primary wage earners and the secondary wage earners? The authors say the answer to this question must come from the courts. Feminist readers will know immediately where they stand on the question since they know who those secondary earners are and how disadvantaged they already are.

33. **Cook, Alice H. "Sex Discrimination at Universities: An Ombudsman's View."** *AAUP Bulletin* 58, 3 (September 1972): 279–82.

From 1969 to 1971, Alice Cook, now professor emerita of industrial and labor relations at Cornell, served as the university's first ombudsman. Cook wrote of the complaints she received in her office, which ranged from bad personnel practices affecting lecturers, who are disproportionately female, to problems of equal access to tenure-track jobs to unequal pay for equal work. She mentions a range of solutions to break "some of the traditional hiring molds," which, if they had been implemented, might have saved this Ivy League institution expensive and protracted lawsuits.

34. **"Cornell States Her Case,"** *Cornell Alumni News* 84, 6 (February 1982): 8–11.

This statement was released by the university administration in late 1981 to explain to alumni why it had "undertaken to defend the decisions of its faculties and deans" in the case of the Cornell Eleven. The statement reviews certain aspects of lead plaintiff Donna Zahorik's case, reporting that she was denied tenure in psychology in 1978 based on her qualifications, not her sex. The statement asserts that, contrary to Zahorik's allegation that women are underrepresented on the faculty, "Cornell is well within the mainstream in the Ivy League" and has made "significant progress" in hiring and promoting women. The statement concludes that "alumni should know that the cost of defense is covered by insurances" and that the case is being defended to safeguard the "continued distinction of the faculty." Zahorik's research is dimissed as "unimaginative" and her teaching as "mediocre." No allusion is made to the contention of Zahorik's faculty supporters that her record is better than that of comparable males who were granted tenure, or to the vote by the majority of the faculty of the College of Arts and Sciences present at a special meeting to reappoint Zahorik.

35. **Costain, Anne N. "Eliminating Sex Discrimination in Education: Lobbying for Implementation of Title IX."** *Policy Studies Journal* (Winter 1978): 189–95.

In 1972, Title IX of the Education Amendments Act called for the elimination of sex discrimination in educational institutions receiving federal aid. There was then a three-year delay while opponents and proponents lobbied and held hearings before regulations were put into effect. This author reviews the process by which this government policy was fought against and for during the crucial testing period, which comes, perhaps surprisingly, after the law has been enacted but before it is implemented. A coalition of women's groups is credited with making Title IX a law and finally ensuring that it was implemented. This author emphasizes both the importance of lobbying and the significance of political alliances among the women's groups that worked together.

36. **Cowan, Ruth B. "Legal Barriers to Social Change: The Case of Higher Education."** In *Impact Era: Limitations and Possibilities*, edited by Hazel Greenberg. Millbrae, Calif.: Les Femmes, 1976, pp. 158–93.

Cowan reviews the underrepresentation of women on faculties, on staffs, and in student bodies and summarizes the responses to this picture advanced by defenders of the status quo: underrepresentation is due to women's preferences, discrimination against women in other sectors of society, and women's lack of qualifications. The fourth argument often advanced, Cowan says, is that underrepresentation may be evidence of discrimination, but there are insufficient data. There are ambiguities and confusion as to what discrimination is and what compliance requires. Big institutions have more financial resources and more patience than grievants. Voluntary compliance has not been forthcoming, she observes and quotes Martha E. Peterson, president of Barnard College, as berating fellow administrators for not taking action to correct injustices until they are forced to: "The disgrace of 'affirmative action' is that HEW had to get into it at all." And, Cowan concludes, pressure from women's groups will change American higher education whether or not the institutions finally come into compliance with the laws.

37. **Crocker, Phyllis L.** *Sexual Harassment in Higher Education: An Annotated Bibliography.* New York: National Organization for Women Legal Defense and Education Fund, 1982.

This eighty-item bibliography focuses almost entirely on the problem of professors harassing students on campus. It includes theses, unpublished papers, action kits, directories of activist organizations, articles, the few books on the subject, and bibliographies. Several works deal with the landmark case of *Alexander* v. *Yale* (459 F. Supp. 1 (D. Conn. 1977), *aff'd*, 631 F. 2d 178 (2d Cir. 1980)), which took so long in court that the student plaintiff had graduated by the time the ruling was handed down. There were several items, however, casting light on the controversy of suits and countersuits at Clark University, where Professor Ximena Bunster claimed she had been sexually harassed by a faculty colleague, Sidney Peck. Most of the works reviewed in this bibliography include constructive suggestions on preventing sexual harassment of students and dealing with it when it occurs.

38. **Curtis, Michael. "Title VII: Making Discrimination Victims Whole."** *Willamette Law Journal* 13 (Winter 1976): 109–33.

The author reviews various remedies granted to successful plaintiffs in industry such as back pay and retroactive seniority. But he calls for a more drastic action for Title VII plaintiffs, the "bumping of incumbent employees to make room for the victims of unlawful discrimination." It is doubtful these remedies would be considered for plaintiffs in higher education, given the judiciary's history of deference to academe.

39. **Davis, Ann E. "Women as a Minority Group in Higher Academics."** *American Sociologist* 4, 2 (May 1969): 95–99.

This article was one of the first sociological studies of women sociologists as compared to men. Davis counted the women's names in the directory of the American Sociological Association, tabulated their occupations, and compared the results with the occupations of 385 male members selected at random. Seventy-one percent of the men were in college teaching versus 51 percent of the women; 4 percent were employed by research organizations versus 9 percent of the women; and 9 percent of the men gave no occupation versus 21 percent of the women. She reports that between 1948 and 1964 women earned 18.5 percent of the Ph.D.'s in sociology awarded by the University of California—five degrees.

40. *Discrimination against Women. Hearings before the Special Subcommittee on Education of the Committee on Education and Labor, House of Representatives, Ninety-first Congress.* Parts 1 and 2. Washington, D.C.: U.S. Government Printing Office, 1970.

These hearings were called by Representative Edith Green of Oregon to consider whether or not section 805 of H.R. 16098 would be passed to "prohibit discrimination against women in federally assisted programs and in employment in education; to extend the Equal Pay Act so as to prohibit discrimination in administrative, professional, and executive employment; and to extend the jurisdiction of the U.S. Commission on Civil Rights to include sex." Many articles and speeches were included in the record, as were the full texts of reports on the status of women at Harvard, Cornell, University of Chicago, and eleven other colleges and universities. Virtually all who testified were in favor of the passage of the legislation; their statements are replete with both facts and fervor. A poignant anonymous statement details discouraging and cruel remarks made to women faculty and students, always referred to later as jokes; the employment history of this person alone might have prompted the extension of legal protections to women.

41. **Divine, Thomas M. "Women in the Academy: Sex Discrimination in University Faculty Hiring and Promotion."** *Journal of Law and Education* 5, 4 (October 1976): 429–51.

Universities sometimes defend themselves in court against charges of sex discrimination by saying that they considered qualified women but that men turned out to be the very best candidates. This rationale is based on viewing the hiring process as what this author calls an ordinal model, the process by which, presumably, members of search committees rank each candidate on each of the dimensions they have previously chosen as job relevant. Candidates are ranked in serial order; the difference between number one and number two is the difference between success and failure. Since men tend to underestimate women's abilities and overestimate men's, women candidates will have to be significantly better than men to be hired. This author proposes an alternate model for hiring: the "skill pool" model. Under this model, all candidates who are deemed to meet the standard necessary for full and satisfactory completion of a job performed in the best traditions of a given university, are winnowed out from the incompetents. This does not require lowering standards, the author reiterates. Using the skill pool approach, this author says, erases the difference between "lower" and "higher" level hiring. "Where discrimination is concerned, professors and switchboard operators alike deserve the protection of the courts. In this respect, the university is in no way special." Divine's method is very controversial.

42. **Downey, Peg, with Endy, Daryl. "A Struggle for Academic Equity."** *Graduate Woman* 75, 6 (November-December 1981): 10–15.

This journal, circulated to the 190,000 members of the American Association of University Women (AAUW), announced in its September-October issue that the national organization was inaugurating an advocacy fund, through which members could support academic litigants. As its first project, it will have the case of the Cornell Eleven, five ex-faculty women who are suing Cornell University, claiming sex-based employment discrimination in recruitment, selection, reappointment, promotion to tenure, and equal pay. This article, by two members of the AAUW program staff, details the cases of former assistant professors of psychology, Russian literature, sociology, human service studies, and photography and quotes extensively from the group's legal brief.

43. **Eckert, Ruth E., and Stecklein, John E., "Academic Women."** In *The Professional Woman,* edited by Athena Theodore, Cambridge, Mass.: Schenkman Publishing Company, 1971.

This study of almost two hundred women faculty members in the thirty-two public and private colleges in Minnesota was undertaken in the 1950s, when it was thought that student enrollments would continue to soar. Thus, the authors set out to show how the potential of women as faculty members could be tapped by studying those women who had made it into the college teaching profession. The authors conclude women faculty members need more assistance and encouragement from administrators and colleagues, that women graduate students need more financial support, and that women undergraduates need, most urgently, to be encouraged to enter college teaching. This article first appeared in *Liberal Education* in 1959, when women comprised only 22 percent of the faculty in higher education in Minnesota and nationwide. There has been little change in these proportions. What has changed is that the need for college teachers has diminished drastically and that the women faculty at the University of Minnesota felt themselves so unfairly treated that they filed a class action suit— and won.

44. **Edwards, Harry T., and Nordin, Virginia Davis.** *Higher Education and the Law.* Cambridge, Mass.: Institute for Educational Management, Harvard University, 1979.

A professor of law and a professor of educational administration wrote this definitive source book. There are sections on the university as a legal entity, faculty rights, students' rights, and many sections on compliance with Title IX, the Buckley amendment, which protects students' rights to the privacy of their records, and other pertinent legislation.

45. **Erickson, John R., and McGovern, Katherine Savers, eds.** *Equal Employment Practice Guide.* Washington, D.C.: Federal Bar Association, 1979.

This two-volume work presents articles by lawyers interpreting equal employment legislation; the editors take pains to present opposing points of view so as to provide the reader with a representative sample of current thought. The second volume is a trial manual, organized by phases of the trial process, "Pre-charge to Discovery" and "Discovery to Trial." It gives as an example the case of plaintiff Joannie Caucus who has for counsel Perry Mason of 10 Rich Street. In following the development of the case Caucus brings against Fairlie Equal Phumes Corp. (FETCO), the lay reader responds with a certain weariness. Much of the argument turns on technical points that have little to do with the merits of Caucus's case. But, as has been observed elsewhere, one side's technicality is the other side's justice. This is the 1979 edition of a guide published annually in conjunction with a conference held by the Equal Employment Opportunity Committee of the Federal Bar Association and the Bureau of National Affairs Education Systems.

46. *Faculty Tenure: A Report and Recommendations by the Commission on Academic Tenure in Higher Education.* San Francisco: Jossey-Bass, 1973.

This book is the result of the work of a commission sponsored by the Association of American Colleges and the American Association of University Professors and funded by the Ford Foundation. The commission reviews the arguments for and against having "an arrangement under which faculty appointments in an institution of higher education are continued until retirement for age or disability, subject to dismissal for adequate cause or unavoidable termination on account of financial exigency or change of institutional program." The commission concludes that the tenure system is worth retaining, but makes forty-seven recommendations for improving the process by which it is granted and maintained. They call for more student participation in decisions to grant tenure; for responsibility for making these difficult decisions to rest with faculty, not administration; for faculty to take responsibility to ensure that procedures are fair and to "minimize reliance on the courts"; for improved methods of measuring and considering teaching ability of candidates; for candidates to be provided with reasons for nonrenewal of appointment in writing; for candidates to have the opportunity to respond and to give more evidence; and other sensible suggestions, including the important one that institutions not rely on "soft" money to fund faculty positions. The commission also cautions that "an institution probably should not allow more than one-half to two-thirds of its faculty to be on tenure appointments. . . . A larger proportion of tenured faculty is likely to curtail opportunities for the appointment and retention of younger faculty, with undesirable effects on institutional vitality; to impede the development of new programs and interdisciplinary work, for which new faculty will be needed; and to diminish opportunities for the recruitment and promotion of increased numbers of women and members of minority groups."

47. **Farley, Jennie. "Academic Recommendations: Males and Females as Judges and Judged."** *AAUP Bulletin* 64, 2 (May 1978): 82–85.

One thousand, one hundred ninety-four letters of recommendation for candidates for faculty posts in women's studies, dating from 1949 to 1977, were coded for mention of teaching ability, research ability, marital status, and physical appearance. Sixty percent of the letters mention teaching; 46 percent, research; 39 percent, marital status; and 10 percent, appearance. Until 1970, more than three-fourths of the letters routinely gave information about marital status; by 1977, only 12 percent did. The applicants were candidates for posts half-time in women's studies and half-time in traditional departments, where research ability is a prime qualification. Half the letters written for these women did not mention ability as researcher, while in contrast a small sample of letters written elsewhere in the university proved to identify virtually every candidate (97 percent) as to his or her scholarly ability to push back the frontiers of knowledge.

48. ———. **"Affirmative Action and the Fight against Negative Response."** *London Times Higher Education Supplement*, April 25, 1980 (No. 392), p. 10.

This overview of the situation of American women faculty members and the reactions to efforts to implement affirmative action was written for a British audience, who are covered by equal opportunity legislation but no affirmative action requirement. One requirement of affirmative recruiting, widespread advertising of faculty openings, was resisted here quite fiercely, but has long been common practice there.

49. ———. **"Coordinating a Women's Conference: Finding Help for Women on Campus."** Mimeographed. August 1981. Available from the author at 112 ILR Extension. Cornell University, Ithaca, NY 14853.

One way academic women can call attention to the problems they encounter is to plan a conference, seeking cosponsorship from the very institutions that are the sources of their troubles, as well as from out-side organizations. They can aim to bring experts to campus to help them resolve their problems. From an institutional perspective, it is better to have a conference than a draining, expensive, prolonged court battle. If the institution can be prevailed upon to provide a forum, would-be antagonists may be able to discuss the issues on neutral turf in a more measured, informed way than would otherwise be the case. The paper provides step-by-step suggestions for planning, developing, funding, and evaluating a conference. Examples of pitfalls unique to women's conferences are included.

50. **Farley, Jennie, ed. "Resolving Sex Discrimination Grievances on Campus: Four Perspectives." Mimeographed. July 1981. Available from the editor at 112 ILR Extension, Cornell University, Ithaca, NY 14853.**

These four papers were delivered at Cornell University in April 1981 as a follow-up to the 1980 conference on sex discrimination in higher education held there. Dianne Brou Fraser, assistant general counsel at Harvard, describes the internal grievance mechanism there and how it was utilized in the case of sociologist Theda Skocpol. Delores Barracano Schmidt, assistant vice chancellor for affirmative action at the State University of New York, describes how the grievance procedure for that sixty-four-campus system was developed and the extent to which it has been used to resolve disputes that otherwise might well have gone to court. Author Joan Abramson describes her case against the University of Hawaii, which has now dragged on for more than ten years, being reviewed and rereviewed in government agencies. Her case is typical of the many grievances she studied at universities and in government all across the country. She was looking for a satisfied customer, a woman who had grieved and was satisified that either a state or federal agency or a court had granted what was due her. In this controversial paper, she reports that she could not find one. Biologist Anne Fausto-Sterling of Brown University discusses the effect on other women at her institution of having a suit filed there (by anthropologist Louise Lamphere) and a consent decree result from it: "The consent decree has changed our lives at Brown. There are more of us, and we have better safeguards than ever before."

51. ———. *Sex Discrimination in Higher Education: Strategies for Equality.* Ithaca, N.Y.: New York State School of Industrial and Labor Relations, 1981.

This book documents a conference held in 1980, "Creative Approaches to Ending Sex Discrimination in Higher Education." It includes papers by attorney Judith Vladeck, an experienced Title VII litigator; Mary P. . .

Rowe of MIT, a well-known mediator of academic disputes; Helen and Robert Davies of the University of Pennsylvania, experts on the problems academic women encounter with internal grievance procedures; and noted activist Bernice Sandler, director of the Project on the Status and Education of Women, Association of American Colleges, who points out the need for concerted action by women academics. The book also includes summaries of the discussion these papers elicited and reports on the status of women, and of grievances, at some twelve other institutions. The Davieses summed up the prevailing sentiment of the conference when they wrote, "It is clearly necessary to improve procedures and morality and thus the chance of justice being done." Attorney Vladeck termed litigation in the courts a failure of creative approaches to these problems. She noted that the women she represents at the State University of New York and at City University of New York had all undertaken protracted efforts to resolve the problems within their institutions before they came to her. To them and to her, litigation was the strategy of last resort.

52. **Farnsworth, Marjorie W.** *The Young Woman's Guide to an Academic Career.* New York: Richards Rosen Press, 1974.

This excellent handbook is aimed at women graduate students in science and engineering, but it is also very useful for the beginning professional. Farnsworth, author of a widely used textbook in genetics, is candid and straightforward. She does not minimize the barriers women will encounter.

53. **Ferber, Marianne; Huber, Joan; and Spitze, Glenna. "Preferences for Men as Bosses and Professionals."** *Social Forces* 52, 2 (December 1979): 466–76.

Does everybody prefer a man boss to a woman? In a survey of 1,402 university staff and academic employees, these researchers asked, "Would you prefer a man or a woman when choosing a _____ [boss, accountant, dentist, lawyer, physician, realtor, veterinarian]?" Other questions elicited information on the extent to which the respondents knew women and men in these capacities and the perceived quality of them. Sixty-four percent of the men and 51 percent of the women preferred men in at least one of the roles, while 17 percent of the men and 30 percent of the women preferred women. Characteristics of persons showing least preference for males were high education, youth, marriage to a professional, and high exposure to professional women. These findings suggest that women are somewhat less prejudiced against women than men are and that the presence of women in male-dominated professions decreases prejudice against them.

54. **Ferber, Marianne A., and Kordick, Betty. "Sex Differentials in the Earnings of Ph.D.s."** *Industrial and Labor Relations Review* 31, 2 (January 1978): 227–38.

Women Ph.D.'s earn less than men. This is often attributed to women's career interruptions; and it is said that once women return to the work force permanently, the gap between their wages and men's decreases. Economists Ferber and Kordick studied thirty-six hundred women and men who had earned their doctorates in the periods of 1958–63 and 1967–72 and rejected both of these hypotheses. "All of our data lead us to reject the proposition that the lower rewards of highly educated women are chiefly caused by their voluntary decision. . . . " Thus this study rejects the human capital model. The authors feel that the evidence "points toward the need for vigorous pursuit of antidiscrimination and affirmative action policies."

55. **Ferber, Marianne A., and Loeb, Jane W. "Performance, Rewards, and Perceptions of Sex Discrimination among Male and Female Faculty."** *American Journal of Sociology* 78, 4 (January 1973): 995–1002.

At the University of Illinois 139 women and 139 men matched by department and rank were surveyed in 1970. In this sample, married women proved to be no less productive than single ones, yet appear to experience less success in academic life. Marital status was the best single predictor of perception of sex discrimination for women, i.e., married women were more likely to report unequal opportunities for women in their respective departments than single women were. Women as a group were more likely to report lack of equal opportunity for women than men were. Among men, the least likely to report perceiving sex discrimination were the most successful. In this sample, faculty wives tended to be employed in predominantly male fields. This, the authors say, suggests that the predominantly female fields on the campus may be "particularly disinclined to give regular appointments to faculty wives, perhaps because of the relatively large numbers of women asking them to do so."

56. **Ferber, Marianne A., and McMahon, Walter W. "Women's Expected Earnings and Their Investment in Higher Education."** *Journal of Human Resources* 14, 3 (Summer 1979): 405–20.

A survey of 2,580 students who were freshmen in fall 1972, and their families, included a question on expected earnings after graduation and a request that the student estimate what he or she will be earning in twenty-five years. Women expected to earn at least as much and often more than men. The authors admit the possibility that the women may be disappointed, but conclude on balance that "women's high expectations, high investment in education, especially in formerly male-dominated fields, increasing labor force participation, and decreasing fertility all tend to reinforce each other so as to create a 'benign circle', and all contribute toward reducing the female-male earnings gap."

57. **Ferber, Marianne A., and Westmuller, Anne. "Sex and Race Differences in Nonacademic Wages on a University Campus."** *Journal of Human Resources* 11, 3: 366–73.

The authors studied the forty-eight hundred nonacademic employees at the Urbana-Champaign campus of the University of Illinois and concluded that sex and race of worker significantly influence the pattern of wage rates and earnings by occupation. Comparing the four race and sex categories, these authors show that majority males and minority females appear to gain most salary advantage from additional education.

58. **Fidell, L. S. "Empirical Verification of Sex Discrimination in Hiring Practices in Psychology."** *American Psychologist* 25, 12 (December 1970): 1094–98.

The author sent out descriptions of ten individuals, which purported to describe real people, to the chair of each of the 228 graduate psychology departments in the United States. The cover letter asked the respondents to "judge your *current* impression about the chances of his getting an offer for a full-time position." When the respondent thought the person described was female, he or she reported that she would be hired at a lower level than a person described as male. Men received more tenure-track position offers than women; only men were offered full professorships. The modal offer reported for women was assistant professor; for men, associate professor.

59. **Fields, Rona M. "The Status of Women in Psychology: How Many and How Come?"** In *Who Discriminates against Women?* edited by Florence Denmark. Beverly Hills, Calif.: Sage, 1974, pp. 95–123.

Between 1968 and 1972, there was no improvement in the status of women in psychology. The authors review the efforts made by professional groups and find them wanting. Many tables.

60. **Flygare, Thomas.** *"Board of Trustees of Keene State College* v. *Sweeney:* **Implications for the Future of Peer Review in Faculty Personnel Decisions."** *Journal of College and University Law* 7, 1–2 (1980–81): 100–10.

The case of Christine Sweeney is, according to this author, the first in higher education where a court overruled a unanimous peer recommendation against promotion or tenure. Sweeney's application for promotion to full professor was unanimously supported by her department colleagues and unanimously rejected by the five members of the faculty evaluation advisory committee at Keene State. Flygare reviews this court decision favoring Sweeney and other related decisions to show that judges are beginning to abandon their hands-off attitudes toward academic institutions. "If administrators and governing boards can no longer rely on a peer review recommendation—even a unanimous recommendation—as an adequate defense in a Title VII suit, then there may be some who would suggest eliminating peer review altogether." But, this author continues, what these decisions teach us is that the peer review process needs improvement: "Evaluation standards need to be clearer and more objective. Methods of measuring performance against those standards need to be refined. The frequency and timeliness of various components of the evaluation process need to be studied."

61. **Foegen, J. H. "Double-Dipping the Labor Market: Sex-Bias Cause?"** *Labor Law Journal* 30, 3 (March 1979): 180–82.

Why do men resent working women? Because, this author suggests, they fear that women are taking jobs away from male breadwinners in order to supplement their husbands' incomes. He notes that, due to government regulation, "being a woman is a definite asset" in job hunting. The working woman is resented, he says, not because of her sex but because she is part of the two-earner family. And, he speculates, one way to get rid of this problem would be to legislate one job per family in hard times. (See also *Baldwin*.)

62. **Ford Foundation.** *Women in the World: A Ford Foundation Position Paper.* New York: Ford Foundation, 1980.

A thirty-six-page report presents the rationale for the Ford Foundation's decision to more than double the investment it is making in programs aimed at advancing women's opportunities in the world. Part 1 describes the effect of sex discrimination on compensation, women's access to credit, the effect on the unemployment rate, the education and training of women for economic roles, and the obstacles to women's participation in the economy. Part 2 describes present and projected Ford Foundation activities. Of particular interest is the passage on page 32 that describes the foundation's commitment to support projects that will assist institutions to comply with Title IX of the Education Amendments Act of 1972 and projects that "examine the possibility of settling disputes through various forms of conflict resolution such as mediation and arbitration."

63. **Fowlkes, Martha R.** *Behind Every Successful Man: Wives of Medicine and Academe.* New York: Columbia University Press, 1980.

A comparison of the effect husbands' work has on the lives of forty women, twenty married to academics and twenty to physicians. The professors' wives tend to be a little better educated, to have had more developed careers at the time of marriage, and to have worked or studied most of their married lives, despite the presence of children, than the doctors' wives. The medical couples met in settings outside the work environment. In contrast, thirteen of the twenty academic couples met in a common work or academic environment. The author's thesis that the husbands could not have been successful without the wives is not, according to one reviewer, supported by the data. Adeline Levine, reviewing the book in the November 28, 1980, issue of *Science*, holds that in order to make that assertion, she would have had to compare these men with unmarried men, or with men married to other kinds of wives, or with those living with roommates or their parents. Fowlkes, however, demonstrates to this reader's satisfaction that the academic wives contributed a great deal to their husbands' success both as wives and as unpaid research assistants. Their own careers were promising when they were married, but only three of the twenty were working full time when interviewed. Ten work part time. This may be by choice, but the anecdotal evidence suggests otherwise.

64. **Fox, Mary Frank.** "Sex Segregation and Salary Structure in Academia." *Sociology of Work and Occupations* 8, 1 (February 1981): 39–60.

This researcher analyzed the male-female pay gap on a university campus to test three hypotheses: that high proportions of women in an academic unit depress men's salaries; that women's salaries are higher in male-dominated units than in female-dominated units; and that men in female-dominated fields are compensated for being there by receiving higher salaries. None of these hypotheses were supported by the data she used from a major midwestern university's personnel records in June 1971. She found that the sex composition of a given unit was not a significant determinant of salary but that achievement was. That is, academic units with higher proportions of female employees with doctorates or with six or more years seniority had higher women's salaries. The author entertains the idea that the entry of high-achieving women into a discipline may, however, depreciate the status of the field so that men with less distinguished credentials may be recruited. Alternatively, she says, it may be that when an occupation or discipline declines in importance and status, high-achieving males may move on, leaving room for females. Either way, as women move in, there goes the neighborhood.

65. **Francis, Lesley Lee. "Litigation on Sex Discrimination: An Update."** *Academe* 67, 4 (August 1981): 294–95.

This concise report summarizes recent court decisions affecting women academics and recent activities of the American Association of University Professors (AAUP). One of the association's committees, "Committee W," is concerned with the status of women in the academic profession. That committee met in March 1981 to express its concern for the rights of persons who may have been discriminated against. "It drew attention to the particular problems of faculty members who allege discrimination in personnnel decisions at institutions where internal procedures are inadequate or non-existent and the heavy burden faculty members must assume if they decide to pursue a discrimination case in the courts. Recognizing the overriding need to eliminate bias in decisions affecting faculty status, Committee W urged greater accountability for those involved in the decision-making process."

66. **Franklin, Phyllis; Moglen, Helene; Zatlin-Boring, Phyllis; and Angress, Ruth.** *Sexual and Gender Harassment in the Academy: A Guide for Faculty, Students, and Administrators.* New York: Modern Language Association of America, 1981.

This seventy-four-page book is the best short discussion yet of what sexual harassment is; how it appears to affect women as students, staff, and faculty; how colleges can best deal with it when it arises; and what the law requires. According to these authors, when a person in authority presses unwanted sexual attention on a subordinate, he or she is guilty of sexual harassment, especially when it appears that institutionally inappropriate rewards or penalties may result from compliance or refusal to comply. They define gender harassment as verbal harassment or abuse, often in public settings, of women as a group. They discuss, in a reasonable and low-key manner, how both kinds of behavior can corrupt institutional integrity, detract from a healthy learning and working environment, and do damage to women. Included are discussions of romantic affairs that are seemingly consensual, the difference between looking at a woman and ogling her, the extent to which a professor is free to make jokes or remarks about women in his or her classroom without worrying about the effect on women students, and the effects of the sexual harassment of junior faculty in English or foreign-language departments "with or without literary allusion." Throughout this carefully written text are helpful examples of institutional response to the problem, ranging from Rutgers University's decision to publish its policy on sexual harassment in the course roster each term to MIT's delicate statement that, while the institute does not intend to "interfere with the course of true love," faculty members or teaching assistants should divest themselves of educational or supervisory responsibility for employees, faculty members, or staff members when personal relationships develop with them. There is a fifty-item bibliography and an appendix with sample procedures and policies from University of Iowa, University of California at Santa Cruz, Rutgers, Stanford, University of Washington, Yale, and Duke.

67. **Friedman, Joel William. "Congress, the Courts, and Sex-Based Employment Discrimination in Higher Education."** *Vanderbilt Law Review* 34, 1 (January 1981): 37–69.

At the end of the nineteenth century, women constituted 20 percent of all university and college faculty members, according to Friedman. By 1939, they accounted for a record 27.6 percent, but had dropped back to 25.4 percent by 1977. Despite the enactment of Title VII of the Civil Rights Act of 1964 and of Title IX of the Education Amendments Act of 1972, women are still not adequately protected against the "sexually discriminatory employment practices of institutions of higher education." This law professor believes that the problem can be traced directly to judges and documents his assertions persuasively. He reviews theories of sex discrimination as they can be applied to academic institutions and cites judicial decisions on numerous Title VII and Title IX cases to show that "the federal courts have frustrated Congress's effort by adopting an extremely passive approach to challenges raised against university employment decisions."

68. **Fritschner, Linda Marie. "Women's Work and Women's Education: The Case of Home Economics, 1870–1920."** *Sociology of Work and Occupations* 4, 2 (May 1977): 209–34.

The author traces women's movement into the industrial work force and the rise of home economics education both in the Northeast and in the Midwest. She labels the latter movement a "backward-looking" response to social change, as one of its aims was to divert women from outside employment. This historical analysis adds perspective to the current effort to encourage integration of male faculty and male students into the field of home economics.

69. **Furniss, W. Todd, and Graham, Patricia Albjerg, eds.** *Women in Higher Education.* Washington, D.C.: American Council on Education, 1974.

This volume contains some three dozen chapters on the situation of women in academic life, including sound suggestions for change.

Among the most interesting are Katherine M. Klotzburger's essay on the role of the affirmative action advisory committee; Robben W. Fleming's candid discussion of why it is hard to implement affirmative action at the University of Michigan; Ann L. Fuller's remarks on the status of the administrator's wife; Jacquelyn A. Mattfeld's analysis of the role women play in administering Ivy League institutions; and Heather Sigworth's discussion of the effect of antinepotism rules on women on campus. One unintended but unfortunate note is struck in the concluding essay in the volume by Roger W. Heyns, president of the American Council on Education. He writes that in addition to its three most urgent tasks, the council and educational leadership will also "deal with important but subsidiary problems" such as "responding more adequately to women and ethnic minorities."

70. **"Future of EEOC and Norton Resignation."** *Labor Relations Reporter*, February 2, 1981 (no. 106), pp. 84–86.

This article summarizes the 150-page transition team report on the future of the Equal Employment Opportunity Commission submitted to President Ronald Reagan. The report concludes, "EEOC has, rather than implementing the 1964 Civil Rights Act against racial and other forms of discrimination, created a new racism in America, in which every individual is judged by race and every employer must keep records on the basis of race, sex, and other such criteria." According to this summary, the report attacks EEOC's interpretation of Title VII as applied to discriminatory intent, testing, and affirmative action, but makes no reconciliation between its positions and U. S. Supreme Court rulings such as *Griggs* v. *Duke Power Co.* (401 U.S. 424, 432 (1971)) and *Weber* v. *Kaiser Aluminum* (611 Fed. 132), which have endorsed the commission's stand. The transition team report calls for a reconsideration of the entire philosophy of affirmative action, which, it is noted, is found no place in legal statutes but only in an executive order and administrative regulations.

71. **Gappa, Judith M., and Uehling, Barbara S., *Women in Academe: Steps to Greater Equality.*** Washington, D.C.: ERIC Clearinghouse on Higher Education, George Washington University, 1979.

After reviewing the literature on the status of women students, staff, and faculty, the authors make five recommendations for change: (1) expand the information base; (2) provide incentives for change; (3) eliminate institutional barriers (aspects of the screening process used to winnow out candidates for faculty posts that have disparate effects on males and females); (4) provide new institutional services; and (5) review progress continuously and take necessary action.

72. **Geis, Florence L.; Carter, Mae R.; and Butler-Thompson, Dore, "Seeing and Evaluating People."** Mimeographed. Newark, Del.: Office of Women's Affairs, University of Delaware, 1981.

This crisp report summarizes what is known about sex-biased perception, evaluation, and stereotyping. Its purpose is to inform administrators and faculty about the ways in which discrimination against women continues in spite of sincere beliefs in equality of opportunity on the part of decision-makers. The authors highlight their research summary with telling subheadings: "Women's work is not only devalued upon completion, it is performed with less support from the beginning" and "The professional woman's dilemma is often between being undervalued if she remains polite and accommodating, and being punished if she doesn't." The report concludes with solid recommendations that the authors hope administrators, department chairs, and faculty members will implement. It is an unusual blend of widely accepted findings of social psychological research and new feminist work. It is carefully documented with no fewer than eighty-three references.

73. **Gellhorn, Ernest, and Boyer, Barry B. "Government and Education: The University as a Regulated Industry."** *Arizona State Law Journal 77,* 1 (February 1973): 569–97.

These authors, who are at once faculty members, attorneys, and deans, present an interesting comment on the growth of regulation and its effect on institutions of higher education. They note that the university as an employer can sometimes dominate a community and contend that the government intervention has not been altogether bad—a view seldom aired. It is not surprising, they say, that "given the extraordinary record of abuses of public trust by powerful institutions inside and outside government during the past decade, the public's view of institutional power is heavily colored with skepticism and suspicion. The large amounts of public money flowing into higher education probably would have brought a demand for greater controls on the use of those funds in any event. Still, the academic community reacts with surprise and resentment to this questioning of its integrity." One difficulty with affirmative action, they note, is that the only sanction, cut-off of federal funds, is too strong. Overall, they hold that the growing interaction with regulatory agencies could be an opportunity rather than a threat. It at least provides the opportunity for educators to redefine for themselves what the central missions of their institutions are to be.

74. **George, Diana Hume. "The Miltonic Ideal: A Paradigm for the Structure of Relations between Men and Women in Academia."** *College English* 40, 8 (April 1979): 864–70.

Male academics seldom permit themselves to say that women are innately inferior or that woman's place is in the home. But, according to this author, many of them still share the Miltonic notion that, in the hierarchy of beings, woman ranks below man and that her pretense to intellectual parity is exactly that—a pretense. Men are made anxious by women's entry into the professoriate. They do permit themselves to complain about what they term feminist defensiveness and about words like "chairperson." And they do share stories about worthy male candidates losing out to less worthy females because they "needed a woman." In fact, this author says, "Many male academics harbor the conviction that most of their female colleagues are not, intellectually, quite up to snuff. Affirmative action horror stories provide them with one relatively safe way to say so." She concludes gloomily that so long as the Miltonic male "unaware of the paradoxes of his wishes and fears" dominates academe, the relationship between men and women professors will continue to be tense and inhibited.

75. **Ginensky, Amy B., and Rogoff, Andrew B. "Subjective Employment Criteria and the Future of Title VII in Professional Jobs."** *Journal of Urban Law* 54 (1976): 165–236.

The authors, in a seventy-page article with more than three hundred footnotes, establish beyond reasonable doubt that in Title VII cases courts require clearer, more convincing, and more specific statistical evidence from white-collar plaintiffs than from blue-collar plaintiffs. They show that, in university cases involving sex discrimination claims, judges are very likely to permit institutions to rely on subjective criteria in evaluating academic performance. So long as that is the case, they say, Title VII "represents an illusory promise to professional employees." One quirk in the system is that while the evaluator's race or sex is not seen as an acceptable reason to challenge an employment decision, it has been accepted as evidence to support one. Given these discouragements, how should lawyers argue for plaintiffs in Title VII cases? The authors provide some interesting tips.

76. **Ginsberg, Eli; Berg, Ivar E.; Brown, Carol A.; Herma, John L.; Yohalem, Alice M.; and Gorelick, Sherry.** *Life Styles of Educated Women.* New York: Columbia University Press, 1966.

This book reports a study of the careers and attitudes of 311 women who held fellowships at Columbia University after World War II. The authors marveled at the ingenuity with which these talented women had been able to manage both careers and family responsibilities. They report that 7 percent felt that their sex had helped them in their careers, while 33 percent reported having encountered sex discrimination. Policy implication? Parents can know that their daughters may encounter some barriers because of their sex, but these will be only a "minor hindrance." In spite of this misperception, the authors do make valuable, if rather vague, suggestions for ways in which private employers, educational institutions, and the government could nurture female talent. Presumably, if they had been implemented, these suggestions would have helped all women, not only the supertalented ones who were able to work even though they were mothers.

77. **Gleason, George. "The Job Market for Women: A Department Chairman's View."** In *A Case for Equity: Women in English Departments,* edited by Susan McAllister. Urbana, Ill.: National Council of Teachers of English, 1971, pp. 81–88.

This article is based on a paper delivered at the Modern Language Association's 1970 meetings. Identifying himself as chairman of the department of English at South West Missouri State, this author states that he has sought to balance his teaching staff by sex and lists the academic ranks and gives the numbers of women and men at each level from instructor to professor. He describes problems he has had with women faculty, including the fact that few seem to understand that a Ph.D. is a prerequisite for a tenured post today. Many create problems for themselves by marrying, he said, and then are constricted in their progress toward a graduate degree by their family responsibilities and by their lack of mobility. "There are," he concludes, "undoubtedly a few schools where women, like the Irish, need not apply, but all the evidence I have is that the job market in colleges is just as open to women as it is to men." In a response, Mary Anne Ferguson points out that he has left out of his faculty list the women teaching part-time in his department and that his department has an interesting history: there were no male faculty there until 1938, and now 75 percent of the senior faculty are male. Why are women in "the basement"? It is due, she says, to the "hostility and rigidity of academe rather than women's lack of will."

78. **Goldberg, Philip A. "Prejudice toward Women: Some Personality Correlates."** In *Who Discriminates against Women?,* edited by Florence Denmark. Beverly Hills, Calif.: Sage, 1974, pp. 55–65.

In 1968, psychologist Goldberg showed two groups of women identical scholarly essays. Half were led to believe the essays were by women and half by men. The work purportedly written by men was judged to be significantly better than the identical work by women. Goldberg reviews these and other studies that give objective evidence of prejudice against women to try to ascertain if misogynists differ from other people in significant ways. He reviews study after study and concludes that the reason he cannot find correlates is that misogyny approaches being a cultural universal.

79. **Goldstein, Elyse. "Effect of Same-Sex and Cross-Sex Role Models on the Subsequent Academic Productivity of Scholars."** *American Psychologist* 34, 5 (May 1979): 407–10.

This ingenious researcher tabulated the number of articles published by 110 persons who earned the Ph.D. in psychology at City University of New York, the New School for Social Research, and New York University between 1965 and 1973. She hypothesized that the publication rate of those who had Ph.D. advisors of their own sex might be higher than that of those who had advisors of the opposite sex. Her data support this hypothesis.

80. **Gordon, Margaret, and Kerr, Clark. "University Behavior and Policies: Where Are the Women and Why?"** In *The Higher Education of Women: Essays in Honor of Rosemary Park,* edited by Helen S. Astin and Werner Z. Hirsch. New York: Praeger, 1978, pp. 113–32.

This book is a tribute to educator Rosemary Clark, former president of Connecticut College, Barnard College, and vice chancellor of UCLA. It is a collection by her colleagues of essays and studies, of which the most interesting is by the associate director and the chairman of the Carnegie Council. Their study permits comparison of one's own institution with others in terms of number of women on the faculty, percent of the full professors who are women, and the proportion of women faculty compared to representation of women among students. Women faculty do least well at the most prestigious universities. In speculating about the future, the authors note that women are best represented in the specialties where the job prospects are most bleak; changes tend to be most pronounced in institutions that formerly had the fewest women on their faculties. They advise universities to make "strong efforts to overcome the effects of past discrimination." The critical question of whether "proportions of women in the high ranks will rise appreciably cannot be answered until the early 1980's."

81. **Gorton, Arlene E., and Wessen, Albert F. "The Lamphere Settlement: A Faculty View."** *Brown Alumni Monthly* 78, 4 (November 1977): 25–37.

Anthropologist Louise Lamphere was not awarded tenure at Brown; she filed a complaint on May 10, 1975, and amended it in February

1976, alleging that Brown was engaged in sex discrimination in violation of Title VII. The matter was certified as a class action in July 1976;
the consent decree between Lamphere and Brown was issued fourteen
months later. The decree, according to Lamphere, includes a number of
important reforms that could be instituted without a lawsuit. This article, by an associate professor of physical education and a professor of
sociology at Brown, describes the process by which the university decided to settle the case out of court and exactly how the agreement to
review again the cases of the three plaintiffs and grant them tenure was
implemented. The second, or class action, part of the consent decree
did not require the university to admit guilt, but the institution did
commit itself to "correct previous injustices, if any, and to achieve on
behalf of women full representativeness with respect to faculty employment at Brown University." The authors pose and answer a series of
questions about the significance of the decree. How long will the consent decree be in force? Until Brown has women faculty in proportion
to their availability pool. Does the decree require dilution of academic
excellence or discrimination against male faculty? No. These faculty
authors conclude that "both male and female, tenured and untenured
faculty will benefit from better employment procedures" and that the
general reaction within the university to the out-of-court settlement was
one of relief.

82. **Graham, Patricia Albjerg. "Expansion and Exclusion: A History of
Women in American Higher Education."** *Signs: Journal of Women in
Culture and Society* 3, 4 (1978): 759–73.

In this thoughtful essay, the author traces the democratization of
American higher education, calling attention to the fact that men bene-
fited from it substantially more than women. She notes the image of the
rumpled, forgetful professor, the evolution of normal schools into
teachers' colleges, and the growing emphasis in the most elite institutions on the research mission. "The most prestigious institutions never
considered women for regular faculty positions until well after World
War II." Graham quotes Richard Lester to the effect that the merit
system was working, but she notes the absence of Jews from most
faculties until the 1940s and Catholics from many philosophy and reli-
gion faculties until later than that. In 1870, women constituted 12 percent of the faculty in American institutions of higher education; by
1976, they were 24 percent. By 2070? "Conceivably, the monolithic ideal
of the research university may also be breaking up under the pressure
of new demands for higher education." The pressure for continuing
education may bring about innovation and renewed diversity in higher
education that will benefit men as well as women.

83. ———. **"Women in Academe."** *Science* 169, 3952 (September 25, 1970): 1284–90.

This article was hailed by academic feminists when it appeared. Although the author's explanations for women's low status in academe seem somewhat dated now, her suggested solutions to the problem seem as sensible now as they did then: (1) the presence of women as senior scholars and administrators; (2) provision for part-time professorial appointments; (3) maternity leave; (4) relaxation of antinepotism rules; (5) child care centers; (6) curriculum changes; and (7) monitoring of the status of women on campus. Nevertheless, she concluded, "Difficult as it is for an academic institution to gird for change when danger is not imminent, the present moment is a time when universities can assume the leadership they have so rarely exhibited in these years of confrontation politics."

84. **Guillemin, Jeanne; Holmstrom, Lynda Lytle; and Garvin, Michele. "Judging Competence: Letters of Recommendation for Men and Women Faculties."** *School Review* 87, 2 (February 1979): 157–70.

This article reports on a study of 243 letters of recommendation for 96 candidates for an assistant professorship in sociology at a northeastern university. Content analysis of the letters revealed that there was consensus among the referees that professional competence is defined principally in terms of career performance and potential: intellect, publication, organizational skills, Ph.D. completion, collegial status, and prognosis for career. Evidence in the letters shows that letter writers believe that women are not as good as men in terms of these important factors. There is little evidence that the women are less motivated or intellectually inferior or less competent, but the men seem still to believe that the women will not fit in. So long as they believe that, the authors note, it will be "difficult for women to enter the ranks of professional sociologists and actually enjoy careers in the discipline."

85. **Haber, B. "Why Not the Best and the Brightest? Equal Opportunity vs. Academic Freedom."** *Equal Opportunity Forum*, January 1981: 19–25.

A seemingly brilliant woman—Yale Ph.D., postdoctoral grants at Brown and Harvard, articles in leading journals and a book based on her dissertation—was passed over for a tenure-track faculty post at Berkeley in favor of a young man with an unfinished Ph.D. and a single article in press. According to rumor, the woman candidate made the men of the history faculty "uncomfortable." A bright spot in this story is the role played by a determined EEOC investigator without whom, according to this report, this recruitment "peculiarity" would have gone unnoticed and unremarked upon. As it is, the compliance review at

Berkeley goes forward at this writing. This article includes brief summaries of the suits at the University of Georgia and the University of Minnesota. The author ends on a criticism of James Dinnan at the University of Georgia for invoking academic freedom as a battle cry against equal opportunity: "The Dinnans of academia are abusing a fragile tool for the sake of their self-serving intolerance."

86. **Hacker, Helen Mayer. "Women as a Minority Group: Twenty Years Later."** In *Who Discriminates against Women?*, edited by Florence Denmark. Beverly Hills, Calif.: Sage, 1974, pp. 124–34.

In October 1951, sociologist Hacker wrote an article advancing the thesis that women fulfilled many of the classical requirements for being classified as a minority group. As a group, they were discriminated against, even though there was little consciousness of it among women. According to her, the article was viewed as "quirky" at the time. In 1971, Hacker reviewed the growth of the women's movement and analyzed three trends: the radical tendency toward female separatism; the resistance to equality on the part of certain privileged women; and the feminine self-image, which, like the defeatist attitudes of other minority groups, permits acceptance of dependent status. As before, this author is way ahead of most analysts in her willingness to talk about things many women do not want to hear.

87. **Hagen, Randi L., and Kahn, Arnold, "Discrimination against Competent Women."** *Journal of Applied Social Psychology* 5, 4 (October-December 1975): 362–76.

The authors report the results of a laboratory experiment undertaken with 120 undergraduates at Iowa State University, of whom half were women. They thought they were taking part in a study of "group predictive abilities," but in fact they were being tested individually for their reactions to having unseen partners. The supposed partners were varied by sex and ability. "This study clearly demonstrates that men, and to some extent women, do discriminate against the competent woman. . . . When deciding which member should be omitted from the group, both men and women showed a tendency to reject the competent woman relative to the competent man."

88. **Hamovitch, William, and Morgenstern, Richard D., "Children and the Productivity of Academic Women."** *Journal of Higher Education* 48, 6 (November-December 1977): 633–45.

Is the number of publications a woman has related to the number of children she has? No, say these authors, who analyzed data on 596 married women Ph.D.'s. They also compared women academics considered outstanding by their peers with other women and found no evidence that child rearing decreases the probability of a woman academic being in the outstanding group. "Many academic administrators have underlying reservations about hiring women faculty due to the belief, whether expressed or not, that those women who may be expected to have children will, as a result, be less productive scholars. Our study provides rather strong evidence that this belief is generally unwarranted and so should not enter into hiring considerations."

89. **Harris, Ann Sutherland. "The Second Sex in Academe."** *AAUP Bulletin* 56, 3 (Fall 1970): 283–95.

In June 1970, this author, then an assistant professor of art history at Columbia, testified before the special House subcommittee on education, advocating the extension of the protection of the 1964 Civil Rights Act to women in higher education. This article, adapted from her testimony, sweeps through the problems of women in academic life, focusing on faculty but alluding to the difficulties encountered by women undergraduates, graduate students, and administrative staff. She relies heavily on several reports from individual colleges: University of Chicago, Berkeley, and Kansas State Teachers College. She quotes at length from the Chicago report and mentions, with careful footnotes, the few discrimination studies that had been done at the time. At the hearings themselves, she noted that she was well aware that the prejudice she described was the result of partly unconscious attitudes and that making laws that forbid sexual discrimination would not solve the problem: "Such laws will help, however, to create the kind of social climate in which men and women can learn to respect each other and learn also not to limit the humanity of each other." (See also *Discrimination against Women*.)

90. *Heritage Foundation Mandate for Leadership: Project Team Report for the Department of Education.* Team chairman, Ron Docksai. Preliminary draft. Washington, D.C.: Heritage Foundation, October 29, 1980.

This report holds that affirmative action does not run counter to American practice, it runs counter to American ideals. Circulated in draft stage, it criticized the *Adams* v. *Califano* (430 F. Supp. 118 (1977)) decision as "outrageous" and singled out the Women's Educational Equity Act of 1974 as an example of bad law badly implemented.

91. **Hill, Herbert. "The Equal Employment Opportunity Acts of 1964 and 1972: A Critical Analysis of the Legislative History and Administration of the Law."** *Industrial Relations Law Journal* 2, 1 (Spring 1977): 1–96.

The author, national labor director of the National Association for the Advancement of Colored People, traces the legislative, administrative, and political problems that impeded the development of the Equal Employment Opportunity Commission into an effective agency. The pre-enactment debate was the longest in the history of our government, he notes; there was opposition from both unions and management. The lack of national support, an increasingly chaotic system of accounting and filing, a basically inadequate enforcement mechanism, plus a ballooning backlog are among the causes he cites for the EEOC's failure. In sum, any groups, including academic women, who look for support of their civil rights from this agency are leaning on what appears to be a very weak reed indeed.

92. **Hoffman, Emily P. "Faculty Salaries: Is There Discrimination by Sex, Race, and Discipline? Additional Evidence."** *American Economic Review* 66, 1 (March 1976): 196–98.

Economists are wont to study sex discrimination in faculty salaries by comparing individuals in terms of age, seniority, education, rank, race, and discipline and explaining away the differentials in terms of those factors. Whatever pay discrepancies still remain may be attributed to discrimination. This author approaches the problem a little differently. She omits rank as a relevant neutral characteristic because, as she notes, women appear to be promoted more slowly than men are. Using her approach, the amount of sex difference in salary that may be attributed to sex discrimination doubles. Aside from that problem, the author says, the human capital model works quite well in explaining salary differences. One wonders if future researchers may not conclude that there are other characteristics now thought to be neutral that are in fact tainted by sex discrimination, for example, discipline. Professors of economics earn more than do professors of home economics. Women trained in economics presumably do not deliberately choose the lower paying subspecialty in all cases. Perhaps some women went to these departments because they were the only departments where they were welcome.

93. **Hoffmann, Leonore, and DeSole, Gloria, eds.** *Careers and Couples: An Academic Question.* New York: Modern Language Association, 1976.

This small book is a collection of essays by women scholars in various disciplines describing the problems they have encountered in being both academics and academic wives. Some observers say that it is an advantage to be in the same field as one's spouse; others say it is a clear disadvantage. The evidence collected here suggests that both arrangements are crippling in academic life and that talent continues to be wasted. *Careers and Couples* is the third in a series of four books sponsored by the Commission on the Status of Women of the Modern Language Association. Hoffmann and DeSole are also the editors of the fourth, *Rocking the Boat: Academic Women and Academic Processes* (1981), which provides the histories of eight women's sex discrimination grievances against their institutions. The contributors emphasize the importance of the support of other women in the ordeal of being rejected and finding the courage to fight back; one fine essay describes how to form "a network of one's own." The only weakness in an otherwise excellent collection results from a decision to withhold the names of most of the institutions where these events took place. This makes it harder for a reader to get in touch with a contributor.

94. **Holahan, Carole Kovalic. "Stress Experienced by Women Doctoral Students, Need for Support, and Occupational Sex Typing: An Interactional View."** *Sex Roles* 5, 4 (1979): 425–36.

Four hundred thirty-seven women graduate students at a large state university were surveyed in 1975. Women in the fields where women are few reported most stress and most need for support, and most reported negative attitudes toward women in their departments. The students in those fields reported the male faculty members being most negative toward women, more so than male faculty in mixed-sex fields or in traditionally female fields. The study found no difference in attitudes of female faculty.

95. **Hopkins, Elaine B. "Unemployed! An Academic Woman's Saga."** In *Women on Campus: The Unfinished Liberation.* New Rochelle, N.Y.: Change Magazine Press, 1975.

The author was deemed, by her chairman, an excellent teacher; nevertheless, after five years of college teaching, she was fired. Why? "My university [Western Illinois University] didn't say in writing that it wanted 82 percent of its teaching faculty to be male. It simply devised policies, which, given the pattern of women's participation in higher education, guarantee that only token numbers of women will stay there long." An instructor in English, Hopkins was let go because she was pursuing a Ph.D. not in literary criticism but in a field that she believed would make her a better teacher, the teaching of composition and literature. The proportion of women on English faculties will decline, Hopkins predicts, because married women have terrible trouble getting into traditional English departments as graduate students and once there have trouble finishing their dissertations because of family responsibilities. Even if they do finish, they will have to overcome the notions that "a good university cannot hire and/or tenure faculty wives or its own graduates and that it cannot allow persons who began their teaching careers as . . . part-time or temporary faculty to advance up the hierarchy." In a masculine system, they want new blood.

96. **Hornig, Lilli S. "Untenured and Tenuous: The Status of Women Faculty in Academe."** *Annals of the American Academy of Political and Social Science* 448 (March 1980): 115–25.

This definitive paper traces the history of women as faculty members in higher education and presents two concise tables. The conclusions are crisp: "Women occupy the lower reaches of the national pecking order. Disproportionately concentrated in all the untenured and non-tenurable ranks, underpaid at all institutions, in all fields and at all ranks, and overloaded with introductory courses, they contribute a valuable marginal labor supply for colleges and universities." But, the author asks, are the institutions buying the best faculty they can afford? Is it economically or educationally sound to permit occupational sex segregation of men as researchers and women as teachers? Hornig notes that few faculty members concern themselves with the effect this segregation has on curriculum or on women students' aspirations or on the ethical issues involved in the lack of equal opportunity. Administrators are often blamed for these omissions, but "it is faculty members who hold power and exercise leadership in autonomous faculties who are remiss." They make the decision about the composition of the professoriate; "these decisions should reflect a greater concern for the enhancement of education and the improvement of scholarship that may result from greater equity."

97. **Howard, Suzanne.** *But We Shall Persist: A Comparative Research Report on the Status of Women in Academe.* Washington, D.C.: American Association of University Women, 1978.

An update of a 1970 AAUW report, this survey reviews the status of women on 588 campuses as of the academic year 1976–77. Results show that the proportion of women as student leaders (and as students on formerly all-male campuses), as administrators, and as trustees increased in the seven years studied. Only the proportion of women as faculty has stayed virtually the same. In 1973, of 43,974 tenured faculty, 7,033 (16.0 percent) were women; three years later, of 49,310, 8,114 (16.5 percent) were women. The author concludes, "Each of us shares a responsibility to work with campus leaders to push our colleges and universities toward . . . equality." There are carefully prepared tables detailing the extent of change in leadership posts held by student women and representation of women on boards of trustees and charting the movement of women into lower level administrative jobs and some mid-management posts. Also included are lists of responding institutions and a copy of the questionnaire used.

98. **Hunt, Morton. "A Fraud that Shook the World of Science."** *New York Times Magazine,* November 1, 1981, p. 42.

This long article is the story of endocrinologist Vijay Somay, an associate professor at Yale who apparently was in the habit of fudging the data ("smoothing out the curves") used as evidence in his published papers. This might never have come to light, if a junior woman researcher's paper had not been passed to his department for review. The reviewer was the chair of the department, Philip Felig, coauthor of many of Somay's papers. Felig reviewed the woman's paper and recommended that it be rejected; Somay then lifted the paper's framework, the woman's formula, copied her exact words in some passages, used some "smoothed out" data he had purportedly collected, and published the paper in his and Felig's names. The woman, Helena Wachslicht-Rodbard, was outraged, and although the chief of her lab threatened to dismiss her when she persisted in her grievance, she made such a fuss that the two kinds of fraud were uncovered. The senior man, Felig, was deprived of a chairmanship at Columbia for which he had been in line; Somay was banished from Yale. There was much talk in professional societies and some sympathy expressed for Felig because he was said to be guilty by association with his junior collaborator. But neither this article nor any public discussions have focused much on the injustice done to the woman researcher whose work was stolen and who has now retired from research and taken up private practice.

99. *An Inventory of Equal Opportunity Programs Presently at Various National Association of State Universities and Land-Grant Colleges Affiliates and Institutions.* Washington, D.C.: Equal Opportunity Committee, National Association of State Universities and Land-Grant Colleges, 1980.

This publication presents the responses of eighty-two colleges and universities to a survey on the number and kind of equal opportunity programs and innovative affirmative action programs in place in 1980. The reader may want to compare the range of services offered at his or her institution with those of other institutions. The listings also provide ideas for programs, e.g., the establishment of a status of women committee, a management intern program, an outreach effort to recruit older women as students, a women's resource center, and the establishment of a high-level administrator with responsibility for women's issues.

100. **Johnson, George E., and Stafford, Frank P. "Women and the Academic Labor Market."** In *Sex, Discrimination and the Division of Labor*, edited by Cynthia B. Lloyd. New York: Columbia University Press, 1975, pp. 201–19.

The authors, using data from the National Science Foundation Register for 1964 and 1970, compared the salaries of academics in four disciplines—economics, sociology, mathematics, and biology—by sex. The sample is restricted to persons with Ph.D.'s who teach full time in an academic institution. Their conclusion? "While women Ph.D.'s start out at salaries only somewhat lower than those of men, their relative salary position erodes with years of potential experience." Is this due to employer discrimination or to sex differences in acquired skills? The authors lean toward the latter explanation.

101. **Johnson, John D., Jr., and Knapp, Charles L. "Sex Discrimination by Law: A Study in Judicial Perspective."** *New York University Law Review* 46, 4 (October 1971): 675–741.

Two law professors review judicial opinions on cases involving women and give the reader what is essentially an overview of a century of sexism on the bench. They define sexism as a preoccupation with group characteristics and remark that they were surprised at the extent to which the survival of sex discrimination can be attributed to pervasive judicial attitudes. The article reviews cases dealing with women as lawyers, bartenders, wrestlers, administrators of estates, protected workers, patrons of taverns, jurors, candidates for admission to men's colleges, criminals, and divorcees. Of special interest is section IV dealing with sex discrimination cases. The authors note that one explanation for judges having a better record on race than on sex discrimination cases is that they may be able to emphathize with men of another race more readily than with women. The old taboos may make it difficult for a middle-aged male judge to imagine the hardships of a young woman.

102. **Kaschak, Ellyn. "Sex Bias in Student Evaluations of College Professors."** *Psychology of Women Quarterly* 2, 3 (Spring 1978): 235–43.

Fifty female and fifty male college seniors and first-year graduate students were given descriptions of teaching methods and practices of six professors. Half the subjects were given the first three courses with female instructors' names on them and the second three, male instructors' names; the other subjects got the first three descriptions with male names and the second three, female names. The results were analyzed by means of six three-way analyses of variance with sex of students, sex of professors, and the academic field in which the professors were supposed to be teaching as the independent variables. Results showed that subject field did not affect the ratings of male and female professors. Female students rated professors equally, but male students gave male professors higher ratings on virtually every measure. Male students in this sample are "clearly biased by supposedly irrelevant information—the sex of the professor." The authors suggest that "if this sample is at all representative, then the use of student evaluations to assess professors' performance deserves careful reevaluation."

103. **Kehoe, Monika; Spencer, Mary L.; and Speece, Karen, eds.** *Handbook for Women Scholars: Strategies for Success.* San Francisco: Center for Women Scholars, 1981.

This excellent book of 340 pages draws together much information of high value for women academics. The authors outline the status and needs of women in academic life, providing a rich lode of specific information about women's rank, pay, discipline, and prospects. They provide a succinct analysis of the barriers women encounter and report the results of a survey of 1,005 women faculty from various institutions around the country. There are quotations from respondents as to the problems they encounter and the reforms they want to see instituted. There are papers by sociologist Jessie Bernard and psychologist Mary Crawford; philosopher Janice Raymond analyzes the career of theologian Mary Daly. Other useful chapters include advice on seeking funding, on coping with special problems encountered by minority women, and on developing protective strategies. Appendixes include an updated list of officers of professional caucuses in the disciplines, gathered especially for this volume, and useful bibliographies.

104. **Kemerer, Frank R.; Mensel, R. Frank; and Baldridge, J. Victor.** "The Twilight of Informal Faculty Personnel Procedures." *Journal of CUPA* (College and University Personnel Administrators Association) 32, 1 (Spring 1981): 17–25.

What is interesting about this article is not its major thesis, that personnel practices are becoming more regularized and regulated. Instead, it is the implied description of what used to be. For instance, as late as 1971, the majority of all faculty members surveyed had no formalized employment contract. The advent of unionization, the proliferation of state and federal regulations, and judicial support for individual constitutional rights are cited as reasons for increased centralization of decision making. The authors remark that "employees who challenge negative personnel decisions have a relatively easy time finding a forum for their complaint"—obviously the perspective of a personnel administrator, not a grievant.

105. **Knoll, David. "Title IX Sex Discrimination Regulations: Private Colleges and Academic Freedom."** *Urban Law Annual* 13 (1977): 107–37.

This author reviews judicial decisions that suggest to him that private universities "should be allowed discretion in setting their own terms of professional employment."

106. **Konan, Mildred Morton. "On Becoming a Professor."** *Cresset* (Valparaiso University), November 1971: 10–11.

Reflecting on the transition from graduate student to faculty member, this author writes that graduate schools do not prepare the woman Ph.D. for the kinds of questions she will be asked in job interviews. There will be questions on "When are you planning to start a family?"—impossible to answer in such a way as to convince the questioner that you are both committed to your career and a normal woman, by his lights. Another to watch out for: "What does your husband do?"— your mate's occupation will be seen as an indicator of your mobility. If he is well paid your salary may suffer. She predicts that new women professors will be excluded from informal department communications, that male colleagues will express concern about the possibility of your getting pregnant. "So you see," she concludes, "you really don't have it made after all. . . . " She calls for new research, new action, and new personnel policies in academe to provide women with satisfying alternatives to making child rearing a lifelong occupation.

107. **Kreps, Juanita M.** *Sex in the Marketplace: American Women at Work.* Baltimore: Johns Hopkins University Press, 1971.

In a crisp chapter on academic women, Kreps summarizes the studies that had been done by 1970. She includes two tables of special interest: women student leaders in various types of institutions and the representation of women in various types of administrative jobs. Analyzing the various reasons why women might be where they are in academe, she seems to favor one that is dear to economists: women might be making a rational decision not to invest heavily in their own human capital because they know they will not be rewarded as well for their investments as men are. More research is needed, she concludes, to separate the effects of market demand from any discriminatory practices on the part of the employer.

108. ———. **"Women in Academia: Today Is Different."** In *Women in the Professions*, edited by Laurily Keir Epstein. Lexington, Mass.: Lexington Books, 1975.

Midway through the decade of the 1970s, economist Kreps assessed the progress women had made in academic life and found it promising. It reminded her of the breakthroughs achieved during World War II, when women moved rapidly into industrial jobs. But, she cautions in 1975, it would be "unwise to view the prospects of career fulfillment as guaranteed because of the greater acceptance of women professionals." Declines in the economy, she predicts, will be a problem for women. Her prediction has been borne out.

109. **LaNoue, George R. "The Federal Judiciary, Discrimination, and Academic Personnel Policy."** *Policy Studies Journal* 10, 1 (Autumn 1981): 105–23.

The author reviews 133 civil rights decisions issued by the federal judiciary regarding academic personnel policies in the 1970s and concludes that although most individual plaintiffs lost, there is a clear and—to him—hopeful trend in these decisions. Courts are more and more willing to intervene to protect individuals' rights, even though these individuals are employed by universities. Despite the facts that women academics have lost much more often than they have won and that a black grievant has never won an academic decision, "it is apparent that the jurisdictional and procedural impediments to the use of the Equal Pay Act and Title VII of the Civil Rights Act have been cleared away. Even more important the disposition of the courts to treat academic discrimination seriously and to apply conventional civil rights rules has been established."

110. **Ledgerwood, Donna E., and Johnson-Dietz, Sue. "The EEOC's Foray into Sexual Harassment: Interpreting the New Guidelines for Employer Liability."** *Labor Law Journal* 31, 12 (December 1980): 741–44.

In this short article, the authors present an interpretation of the 1980 guidelines on sexual harassment. Sexual harassment is "unwelcome sexual advances, requests for sexual favors, and other verbal or physical conduct of a physical nature." There are three types: when compliance with requests for sexual favors is made a condition of employment, when such compliance results in an employment consequence, or when sexual harassment constitutes offensive job interference. The latter, according to the authors, is the hardest to identify and will probably create the most troublesome issues of employer liability. They note that under certain circumstances, managers can be held responsible for permitting subordinates to sexually harass one another. Suggested approaches for prevention include "affirmatively raising the subject, expressing strong disapproval, developing appropriate sanctions, informing employees of their right to raise and how to raise the issue of harassment under Title VII and developing methods to sensitize all concerned."

111. Lester, Richard A. *Antibias Regulation of Universities: Faculty Problems and Their Solutions.* New York: McGraw-Hill, 1974.

Lester is a critic of affirmative action, which he believes has been implemented by people who do not understand academic life. He marshals evidence to suggest that affirmative action was never needed at universities. His critics do not find his evidence persuasive (Sheila Tobias, *Change*, November 1974; Phyllis Zatlin-Boring, *AAUP Bulletin*, October 1975; Bernice Sandler, *Teachers' College Record*, February 1975; and three attorneys writing in *Women's Rights Law Reporter*, March 1975). Lester defended his book against the critics (*AAUP Bulletin*, Spring 1976; *Change*, March 1975), who in turn responded. The whole exchange shows once again how hard it is to demonstrate the existence of sex discrimination in academic life. If you don't think it exists, you may resist government interference fiercely; if you believe it is there, you may feel that government efforts, even if imperfect, are better than nothing.

112. ———. **"The Equal Pay Boondoggle."** *Change* 7, 7 (September 1975): 33–43.

The Equal Pay Act should not be applied to professors in universities, economist Lester argues, because many universities have a merit system. In addition, market forces, i.e., high demand for certain specialties, account for salary differentials on campus. The Wage and Hour Division of the Department of Labor tries to analyze job content at different levels; this is ill-advised, Lester holds, because assistant professors, associate professors, and full professors may well have the same "job content" throughout their careers.

113. ———. **"Labor-Market Discrimination and Individualized Pay: The Complicated Case of University Faculty."** In *Equal Rights and Industrial Relations*, edited by Farrell E. Bloch et al. Madison, Wis.: Industrial Relations Research Association, 1977.

The author criticizes the way the government has required that the universities establish affirmative action plans, especially numerical goals based on availability. He details the problems in trying to compute availability and points out that the government has done it wrong. Lester finds serious weaknesses in the studies on which the recommendations of the Carnegie Commission on Higher Education were based. He is especially critical of the 125 reports women's groups compiled in the early 1970s on the status of women at 146 campuses. The imposition of numerical goals has resulted in some 150 charges filed by men with the Department of Health, Education, and Welfare, charges of "reverse discrimination." The author seems to find the assertions of men—either as disappointed candidates for tenure or as tenured decision makers—more persuasive than those raised by women in any status.

114. **Liss, Lora. "Affirmative Action Officers: Are They Change Agents?"** *Educational Record* 58, 4 (Fall 1977): 418–28.

Liss presents a candid report of what it is like to be an affirmative action (AA) officer in a time when the law on which the position is based is misunderstood, evaded, or resisted. Citing a study of 133 persons in those positions, Liss notes that nearly half were serving part time, and 40 percent were new to the institution when they took on the job. She bases her comments also on her own experience as AA officer at Lehigh and a participant in the then newly formed American Association of Affirmative Action officers. AA officers are seen as cops by faculty members, she says, and as robbers as well, because they have to monitor behavior and are seen as stealing the jealously guarded prerogative of hiring without scrutiny. Some women and minorities see AA officers as puppets of the administration, while administrators see them as far too sympathetic to the "outs." Liss concludes her analysis: " . . . one model for action would be the affirmative action officer reporting the many evasions, cover-ups, and distortions to the compliance agencies." The whistle blower would be protected from retaliation because "harassment is prohibited after complaints are filed."

115. **Lloyd, Cynthia B. "The Division of Labor between the Sexes: A Review."** Introduction to *Sex, Discrimination and the Division of Labor,* edited by Cynthia B. Lloyd. New York: Columbia University Press, 1975, pp. 1–24.

The introduction to this useful book gives a succinct analysis of economists' approaches to explaining the sex segregation of the marketplace and the male-female pay gap. Why are women as a group paid less than men? Among the theories advanced are that they are crowded into the low-paying feminine occupations (Barbara Bergmann); because employers have a "taste for discrimination" (Gary Becker); because they are less productive than men because they have invested less in their own human capital (Jacob Mincer and others).

116. **Loeb, Jane W.; Ferber, Marianne A.; and Lowry, Helen M. "The Effectiveness of Affirmative Action for Women."** *Journal of Higher Education* 49, 3 (1978): 218–30.

A review of the national data available on the effectiveness, cost, and need for affirmative action for women in higher education. The authors compare the status of 137 faculty women with that of 137 comparable men at the University of Illinois in 1969 and again in 1974. They conclude, "The present study documents the failure of an approved affirmative action program to decrease the residual salary difference that exists between men and women after a number of merit and experience indices are accounted for." Their evidence shows, they say, that "procedural compliance does not guarantee results," and they advocate that an incentive approach rather than a regulatory one should be tried. "Governmental regulation . . . has been largely ineffective. It has created costs and backlash but has been too weakly enforced to bring about significant results."

117. **Lunneborg, Patricia W., and Lillie, Carol. "Sexism in Graduate Admissions: The Letter of Recommendation."** *American Psychologist,* 28, 2 (February 1973): 187–89.

Letters of recommendation written for the 123 students admitted to a graduate program in psychology at the University of Washington from 1963 to 1967 were studied. Comments the coders classified as sexist were made about one of the eighty-five men and about eleven of the thirty-five women. The authors note that they know from an earlier study that women in the first four years of graduate work did drop out significantly more often than men did. "If sex stereotype expectations can be changed . . . [and]women not evaluated in terms irrelevant to their success and contribution to psychology, it could be expected that greater numbers of them would persist. . . . "

118. **McCarthy, Jane, with Ladimer, Irving.** *Resolving Faculty Disputes.* New York: American Arbitration Association, 1981.

This eighty-page paperback book is based on the premise that academic administrators and faculty members should be working, not at cross-purposes but together, to fashion procedures for resolving faculty grievances. According to the preface, there are four essential components of such procedures: accessibility, simplicity in administration, prompt resolution, and opportunity for independent review. The authors include model grievance procedures to encourage faculty and administration dialogue.

119. McGuigan, Dorothy G. *The Dangerous Experiment: 100 Years of Women at the University of Michigan.* Ann Arbor, Mich.: Center for the Continuing Education of Women, 1970.

This is a fascinating short history of the first century of coeducation at the University of Michigan. In 1870, the *New York Times* editorialized that "Harvard and Yale, which have so long hesitated on the brink [of coeducation] will have an opportunity to observe the effect on those who have plunged boldly in." Harvard and Yale were, of course, to remain on "the brink" for another century. In 1970, according to McGuigan, the University of Michigan was still not a real community of scholars—it was a fraternity. Such assertions are carefully documented.

120. MacKinnon, Catherine. *Sexual Harassment of Working Women.* New Haven: Yale University Press, 1979.

This long, tightly reasoned book describes and analyzes the nature of sexual harassment and the extent to which working women suffer from it. The author argues what may seem intuitively obvious to the reader, that sexual harassment is in fact discrimination on the basis of sex and therefore that victims can be said to be protected from it by both the Fourteenth Amendment and by Title VII. The argument is written by a lawyer for other lawyers, but it is accessible to the layperson who is not a casual but a careful, patient, reader.

121. Mackie, Marlene. "Students' Perceptions of Female Professors." *Journal of Vocational Behavior*, 8 (1976): 337–48.

The researcher distributed questionnaires to 181 undergraduate and graduate students in sociology at the University of Calgary to test the hypothesis that male professors would be reported to be more competent than female professors and less effective in the "socio-emotional" sphere. In fact, the students said they perceived women teachers as more competent than males as well as more effective socially.

122. Maggarrell, Jack. "Colleges Give Bigger Raises to Women but Men's Average Pay Is Still Higher." *Chronicle of Higher Education* 21, 16 (December 8, 1980): 1,6.

In a survey done for the *Chronicle*'s editors, salary data were gathered in fall 1980 from 2,400 persons in a sample of 4,800 full-time faculty members in American colleges and universities. Results show that American institutions "gave bigger pay increases to women than to men on their faculties [during the last academic year] but the women's average pay remains substantially lower than the men's." Among instructors, women earn 18 percent less than men; among assistant professors, 7 percent; among associate professors, 4 percent; and among full professors, 9.5 percent. Of course, the size of the gap varies by discipline as well, being widest in business, economics, and the humanities and narrowest, surprisingly, in physical education. A letter to the editor in the February 2, 1981, *Chronicle of Higher Education* commented that the title of this article is misleading. "The data show," wrote Nancy J. VanDerveer, research coordinator, John Minter Associates, Boulder, Colorado, "that women's raises are bigger only in the sense of being a larger proportion of their smaller salaries. . . . Last year, the size of the salary gap was $4,083 . . . [Now it is] $4,296 or $213 larger than it was before." VanDerveer concludes, "Them that has, gets."

123. **Martin, Donna. "The Wives of Academe."** In *Women on Campus: The Unfinished Liberation.* New Rochelle, N.Y.: *Change* Magazine Press, 1975.

"Faculty wives may well represent the most highly educated and underutilized source of womanpower in the country," according to this author. "The Ph.D. or near Ph.D. faculty wife accompanies her husband to a college or university and, because of the prevailing rules, a lack of openings in her field or simply because of a petty desire on the part of the administration to prevent any faculty family from earning a double income, is unable to get a job." How to resolve the problem? According to Martin, the wives can lower their career aspirations; the husbands can follow their wives to places where jobs are more plentiful; the institutions can change their policies. Or, most promising perhaps, the women can pressure the government to enforce the laws that make discrimination on the basis of marital status illegal.

124. **Marwell, Gerald; Rosenfeld, Rachel; and Spilerman, Seymour. "Geographic Constraints on Women's Careers in Academia."** *Science* 205, 4412 (September 21, 1979): 1225–31.

Women academics are more likely to live in big cities than men academics, these authors show. This, combined with other evidence, suggests to them that married women's lack of mobility causes some portion of their low achievement. There are, however, alternative explanations for each element in their reasoning. One reason why 46 percent of the women (versus 32 percent of the men) take their first post-Ph.D. jobs in the area where they received their degrees may have to do with discrimination, not with marital status or presumed unwillingness to move. It is well established that women and minorities have more opportunities where they are individually known; strangers tend to rely more on stereotypes. The authors' data do not tell us *when* the subjects were married, only that they are; women professionals may gravitate to big cities not because they are married and the couple needs two jobs but because they are single. A key weakness in their argument is their failure to provide their data by marital status.

125. **Mattfeld, Jacquelyn A., and Van Aken, Carol G., eds.** *Women and the Scientific Professions: The MIT Symposium on American Women in Science and Engineering.* Cambridge, Mass.: MIT Press, 1965.

This volume is of mainly historical interest. It seems astonishing that, in 1964, there were still talks being given on themes such as "The Case for and against the Employment of Women." The keynote speaker, educator Bruno Bettelheim, set the tone: " . . . we must start with the realization that as much as women want to be good scientists or engineers, they want first and foremost to be womanly companions of men and to be mothers." An industrialist reminded those present that "slip-sticks" are not incompatible with lipsticks, and there were pronouncements about female genius at nurturing and how it would transform the sciences. One participant urged women scientists to take up teaching at the high school level—so ironic to read in 1981 when it is recognized that women who aspired to scientific careers were pretty much confined to high school teaching until recently and high school teaching was too crowded even then for this to be good advice. But MIT was at least thinking about the problem long before most institutions ever noticed it.

126. **Mayes, Sharon S. "Women in Positions of Authority: A Case Study of Changing Sex Roles."** *Signs: Journal of Women in Culture and Society* 4, 3 (Spring 1979): 556–68.

For this study, participant-observers studied male-female relations in small task groups. Of particular interest is the report of male reaction to serving in a group with a woman leader. The author concludes, "Women in nontraditional positions of authority over men and women subordinates evoke different reactions than men in equivalent positions. The resistance to changing sex role behavior on the part of men and women involves the deeply embedded fear that change means chaos and collapse in the norms and behaviors that govern the most sacred areas of everyday life—the family and sexuality."

127. **Miner, Anne A. "The Lesson of Affirmative Action for the Equal Rights Amendment."** In *Impact ERA: Limitations and Possibilities*, edited by Hazel Greenberg. Millbrae, Calif.: Les Femmes, 1976, pp. 85–96.

Does affirmative action in industry work? The question is hard to answer, the author explains, but she tries. There are attitude problems and some difficulties because women do not appear to have the high aspirations of their male counterparts. But the highest obstacles to rapid change in higher education, she believes, are the small numbers hired each year and the low availability of women in certain technical fields, which results, she believes, from past discriminatory practices in education. "Consider a university that hires 50 recent Ph.D.'s each year and has a faculty of 1,000, 100 of whom are women. Say the school concludes that 20% of all Ph.D.'s in relevant fields are women and therefore hires 10 new women each year. Assuming no women ever left the university, it would still take 10 years of such hiring for women to reach a representation equal to their availability: 20%. There is no way to achieve dramatic change other than to hire proportionally more women than exist in the relevant pool."

128. **National Research Council Commission on Human Resources.** *Climbing the Academic Ladder: Doctoral Women Scientists in Academe.* A report to the Office of Science and Technology Policy from the Committee on the Education and Employment of Women in Science and Engineering. Washington, D.C.: National Academy of Sciences, 1979.

This excellent report includes a careful study of the supply of women doctorates in science and engineering and of the constraints they face. The conclusions consist of thirteen recommendations, each one of which, if implemented, could help enormously. They call for enriched federal support for women scientists in teaching colleges, those in off-tenure-track positions at universities, those reentering science at mid-career, and those married to academic men. They urge compliance agencies to require salary information in affirmative action reports and suggest that departments and projects should be paying the price of noncompliance, not whole institutions. They call for special institutional attention to the large numbers of women scientists who are employed as lecturers and, in short, pinpoint a number of problems seldom mentioned by observers outside academic life. In their conclusion, they say tartly that universities have driven up the cost of affirmative action by taking, initially, an adversary position and by their "continuing efforts to claim a form of autonomy to which the use of public funds does not entitle them."

129. **Nielsen, Linda L. "Alchemy in Academe: Survival Strategies for Female Scholars."** Mimeographed. Winston-Salem, N.C.: Department of Educational Psychology, Wake Forest University, 1980.

An educational psychologist was turned down for tenure despite what she believed to be an outstanding record; the decision was later reversed; she is now secure in her job. But she has not forgotten the bitter experience and, in this informal twenty-two-page essay, she tries to analyze what happened and understand how she could have handled it better. Now she wishes she had not been so naïve about excellence being rewarded; she wishes she had not ignored the first warning signals that her colleagues were really prejudiced against women; she wishes she had spoken out firmly and forthrightly. She wishes she had insisted on receiving a written evaluation of her work every year; she also wishes she had been a little less open and candid with the faculty men who did her in. She wishes now that she had joined with other women and been open with them, instead. What did she do that she is glad of? She kept records very carefully; she trusted her intuition; she refrained from blaming herself for things that were clearly not her fault.

130. **Nieva, Veronica F., and Gutek, Barbara A. "Sex Effects on Evaluation."** *Academy of Management Review* 5, 2 (1980): 267–76.

If subjects are shown sets of identical credentials, half labeled with a man's name and half with a woman's, will they rate the candidates' abilities and prospects the same? Nieva and Gutek reviewed some fifty studies of evaluation bias and concluded that while a few studies show no difference in the ratings and a few show that the subjects favor women, the majority show that both men and women will rate a subject's performance or credentials higher if they think the candidate is male. The likelihood that bias will be present increases as the amount of information present decreases; the likelihood of bias increases where there is sex role incongruency—for instance, a woman in a "man's" field is more likely to be a victim of prejudice than a woman doing a job seen as appropriate to her sex role; and the higher level the job, the more likely sex bias will be present.

131. **O'Connor, Kathleen. "Why Don't Women Publish More Journal Articles?"** *Chronicle of Higher Education* 21, 11 (November 3, 1980): 25.

This essay is a somewhat light-hearted look at a serious question: Why are journal article authors so seldom women? The author considers the idea that women may fear success or fear failure or have too high standards of perfection. In the December 15 issue of the *Chronicle*, two readers respond. Lynnette Carpenter writes that there is some truth to O'Connor's assertion about women's lack of self-confidence since few women have been given the support in intellectual development that their male counterparts have. Carpenter also cites other factors: most women are still stalled in low-level jobs where there are few opportunities and little free time for writing; many women specialize in topics related to women and gender, which male colleagues dismiss as frivolous and ephemeral; and the very males who are denying tenure to women scholars are the ones controlling access to publication in prestigious journals. She also observes that women, whether scholars or not, still carry most of the responsibility for home care and child care and that it is a challenge, to say the least, to publish as well. Elizabeth V. Swenson notes that O'Connor may have had her tongue in cheek in presenting the ideas in her original essay. But, Swenson writes, "speculating, even facetiously, on motives such as fear of rejection or self-exposure does nothing to dispell common stereotypes of the self-deprecating, struggling, obsequious female academic." Swenson concludes that the low number of publications by females probably reflects the proportion of "publication-relevant jobs" held by women.

132. **On Campus with Women.** Project on the Status and Education of Women, Association of American Colleges, 1818 R Street NW, Washington, D.C. 20009.

This twenty-page quarterly newsletter is a vital source of information about employment trends, the progress of court cases, and innovative ideas for internal settlement. Also available from the Project on the Status and Education of Women are useful publications listing resources for affirmative recruiting, a chart summarizing federal laws and regulations concerning sex discrimination on campus, a series of papers developed to help institutions to accommodate reentry women, and papers on minority women, women in sports, sexual harassment, and other topics.

133. **Patten, Thomas H., Jr. "Pay Discrimination Lawsuits: The Problems of Expert Witnesses and the Effects of the Discovery Process."** *Personnel*, November-December 1978: 27–34.

How can corporations defend themselves against pay discrimination lawsuits? The college professor who is called upon as an expert witness may find himself or herself in trouble, this author advises. For one thing, he or she may find in "largely rational job structures occasional departures from equity caused by collective bargaining distortions, compromises whose rationales has long since been forgotten, arbitral decisions, or the remaining innocent sexist and other institutional influences of the past." Second, a case can be demolished by "discovery," the process by which opposing attorneys gather information about one another's cases. He gives the example of "Miss Alpha suing Beta College because she didn't get tenure and because there is a general pattern of sex discrimination at Beta." The case drags on for two years. During the discovery phase, 330 files of professors are made accessible to the plaintiff; more than 50 legal briefs are handed down; depositions are conducted for a year; Beta hires a second law firm; three other women faculty join Miss Alpha. Beta spends $250,000 in direct costs and $150,000 in administrative time, and then the parties settle out of court.

134. Pendergrass, Virginia E., ed. *Women Winning: A Handbook for Action against Sex Discrimination.* Chicago: Nelson-Hall, 1979.

This is a book of reports by women who have attacked sex discrimination in their places of employment, which range from universities to police stations. There are chapters on the extent to which affirmative action officers can help grievants, on attempts to get action from the Equal Employment Opportunity Commission, and a particularly interesting chapter by the editor on "counterparting," the process by which academic women are invited by administrators to choose males with whom their credentials can be compared to check for pay discrepancies. At Florida International University, Pendergrass, an assistant professor, asked that her record be compared to that of a male associate professor, contending that she had been hired at too low a level. The counterparting system, which requires comparison of credentials of persons with the same title, could not allow this claim. She and many other women there found themselves deeply outraged at the way counterparting worked for them. Chapter 13, which includes a consideration of the advantages and disadvantages of suing, concludes, "Women who run away from sex discrimination instead of running to court don't get to run anything. In addition, an immediate reinforcer is the observation that if one woman files a suit, another woman will get hired." Chapter 14 is the story of a woman law student who sued to get equal opportunity to serve as a senate page. She was told that women would reduce the dignity of the Senate by their presence and—this from the judge who heard her case—that the reason she wanted to be a page was to be able to get into the senators' hotel rooms at night. With the assistance of the ACLU, which handled the case up through the Circuit Court of Appeals, she filed suit and won. Chapter 17 consists of wise advice on how to provide personal counseling during sex discrimination actions, which is as useful for concerned colleagues as for professional counselors. The last chapter—not to be missed—is entitled "A Question of Sex: Should Men Be Allowed to Hold Jobs as Patrol Officers?"

135. Peters, Douglas P., and Ceci, Stephen J. "A Manuscript Masquerade: How Well Does the Review Process Work?" *Sciences* 20, 7 (September 1980): 16–19, 35.

These researchers took one article from each of ten psychology journals, invented new authors' names and fictitious institutional affiliations, and resubmitted them to the very journals that had published them eighteen to thirty-two months earlier. None of these journals review blind, that is, without notifying referees of the authors' names and affiliations. Seven of the ten pseudomanuscripts were not detected as repeats and were sent out for review. Of the twenty-two editorial reviews, only four recommended publication. The authors, while cautious in their interpretation of this evidence, believe that the process of review leaves something to be desired. They attribute at least part of the lack of success that these articles had the second time around to the fact that the reviewers were influenced by authors' affiliations: Prestige University versus Unknown College. The implications for women are not remarked upon, but it has been observed elsewhere that one sex is much more likely to be teaching at Unknown College than Prestige University.

136. *Princeton University: Report of the President, April 1980: Coeducation at Princeton.* Supplement to the *Princeton Alumni Weekly* 80, 16 (April 21, 1980).

This long report traces the representation of women at Princeton from the fall of 1969, when they were 4 percent of the student body, to the fall of 1979, when they were 36 percent of the students. Women have done well academically, in fact slightly better than the men. There is pressure for women's studies: a committee is considering that question. Women on the faculty? There were two nontenured and one tenured in 1969; ten years later, ten tenured and forty nontenured. Much of the report is devoted to the great contribution women have made to the cultural life on campus. It is instructive to compare this account with the article in the same issue by Margaret M. Keenan, "The Controversy over Women's Studies," which quotes various women faculty members about the problems they encounter at Princeton.

137. Project on Equal Education Rights. Summary of the Title IX Regulation. Washington, D.C.: Project on Equal Education Rights, 1112 13th St. NW, Washington, D.C. 20005, 1980.

This is a four-page summary—in everyday English—of the section (title) of the 1972 Education Amendments law that bans sex discrimination in all federally assisted education programs. Title IX protects women faculty in physical education programs and has been utilized primarily by them. This project (PEER) also puts out a short guide entitled "Anyone's Guide to Filing a Title IX Complaint" and other useful materials on sex discrimination, mainly that in elementary and secondary schools and vocational education programs.

138. Pullen, Doris L. "The Educational Establishment: Wasted Women." In *Voices of the New Feminism,* edited by Mary Low Thompson, Boston: Beacon Press, 1970.

This book pulls together the first pioneering writing about the situation of women in America as the new feminist movement gathered steam. The chapter by Pullen details the situation of women in higher education in the late 1960s and calls on women's colleges to lead the way in opening new opportunities. She gives a summary of the devastating criticism of women's colleges published in 1968 by the New York Chapter of the National Organization for Women and concludes that "higher education has failed women." Women colleges will go under altogether, the author predicted, unless they are once again pioneers.

139. Ramaley, Judith A., ed. *Covert Discrimination and Women in the Sciences.* Boulder, Colo.: Westview Press, 1978.

This symposium set out to answer the question, Why were almost 50 percent of the women scientists and engineers surveyed by the National Science Foundation unemployed, while only 12 percent of similarly qualified men were? The panelists' answer: discrimination, both overt and covert. With one exception, the papers focus on the academic world. Astronomer Elske v.P. Smith discusses some of the individual and institutional problems faced by women scientists, especially married scholars, concluding with ten suggestions for administrators, psychologist Irene Frieze reviews the literature that suggests strongly that men—and women—evaluate women's work differently than men's; Carol Bonsaro of the U.S. Commission on Civil Rights contributes a solid, well-documented article on the problems of implementing affirmative action in universities, including examples of ways in which institutions sabotage their own efforts. The concluding article by management expert J. Brad Chapman emphasizes how difficult it will be for men in industry to give women an equal opportunity for management posts—ironic to read in 1981, when business has established a far better record for compliance with EEO regulations than the academy.

140. Reeves, Sandra. "Is Brown Guilty of Discrimination against Women Faculty?" *Brown Alumni Monthly* 77, 7 (April 1977): 26–35.

This lengthy article begins with a review of some seven other suits, among them, several class actions, that have been brought by academic women. Describing the background of the suit brought by anthropologist Louise Lamphere, the author notes that Brown had tenured a high proportion of its faculty, 70 percent, and was in the throes of a budget cut. The grievants claimed that Brown resolved its problem of a dwindling number of tenure slots by putting women, and not men, through a "revolving door," i.e., hiring them but never promoting them. The Lamphere case is described in detail: the scholarly record amassed by Lamphere herself; the requirements for her suit being certified as a class action; the process of discovery; the entry of a total of four law firms. The university's arguments are summarized: that universities are special in that each institution and each department within it must be permitted to be the judges of academic excellence of its members; that Lamphere's credentials were such that she was not qualified for promotion to tenure at Brown. The protracted legal proceedings were estimated as costing $150,000, with the note that this might be a "magnificent understatement"—which turned out to be the case. This is a balanced and interesting summary of the background of the Lamphere case.

141. **Remnick, David. "Sexism in the Ivy League."** *Washington Post,* December 2, 1979. p. A10.

This is an account of the troubles at Princeton when eight women came up for tenure and all were turned down. One was psychologist Diane Ruble, who had been recommended by a majority of nine to one in her own department. The next committee, said to have the "last word on tenure decisions," voted her down. Associate professor of classics Janet Martin resigned her post as chairwoman of the women's studies committee over this issue: "'I left because it became clear to me that Princeton had no commitment to women's studies or the tenuring of women except in token numbers.'" According to Remnick, faculty dean Aaron Lemonick responded to his questions as follows: "To say that we discriminate is ridiculous."

142. **Reskin, Barbara F. "Scientific Productivity, Sex and Location in the Institution of Science."** *American Journal of Sociology* 83, 5 (March 1978): 1235–43.

Comparing the productivity of men and women chemists who earned their doctorates between 1955 and 1961, this research concludes that men have slightly more publications than women. "Regression analyses document sex differences in the determinants of productivity, with women's productivity more responsive than men's to prestigious postdoctoral fellowships, employment in tenure-track university positions, and collegial recognition." The author concludes that explanations for these differences should not rely on a priori group differences but rather on the organizational features of science. Rather than claiming that women are less committed, one should look instead to structural explanations such as that given in Rosabeth Moss Kanter's work on the effects of a group's sex composition on its productivity (*Men and Women of the Corporation*. New York: Basic Books, 1977).

143. ———. "Sex Differentiation and the Social Organization of Science." *Sociological Inquiry* 48, 3–4 (1978): 6–37.

This interesting essay draws on anecdotal evidence from women scientists' accounts of their experiences. The evidence suggests that there are obstacles to collegiality between the sexes; this helps to introduce sex differentiation into the scientific community; this in turn will "be manifest in the positions that the sexes typically occupy and in differences in their scientific role performance." The author analyzes such topics as models for cross-gender relationships and sex differences in distribution of recognition. While it is saddening to read about the problems encountered by women scientists including Nobel laureates Maria Goeppert Mayer and Rosalyn Yalow, it is intriguing to read the author's conclusion that "possibly the best situation for a female scientist is marriage to a professional in another discipline. Her marital status would facilitate her social and professional integration, and the disciplinary difference would reduce the chance of her husband's receiving credit for her research contributions."

144. Rossi, Alice S. "Status of Women in Graduate Departments of Sociology, 1968–1969." *American Sociologist* 5, 1 (February 1970): 1–12.

Using data from a survey sponsored by the women's caucus of the American Sociological Association and from one undertaken by the association itself, Rossi traced the flow of women through academic institutions. Her conclusions: women constituted at that time 43 percent of college seniors planning graduate work in sociology; 37 percent of master's candidates in graduate school; 30 percent of Ph.D. candidates in graduate school; 31 percent of graduate students teaching undergraduates; 27 percent of full-time lecturers and instructors; 14 percent of full-time assistant professors; 9 percent of full-time associate professors; 4 percent of full-time full professors; 1 percent of graduate sociology department chairpersons; 0 percent of the 44 full professors in the five elite departments (Berkeley, Chicago, Columbia, Harvard, and Michigan). It is time, she concludes, for academic sociology "to begin a critical appraisal of its own negative impact on the women students and junior faculty members who seek careers in sociology. Comprised of experts in social organization, sociology departments should be in the vanguard in devising institutional arrangements that would permit more women to persist and to advance. . . . " A postscript includes information on the women's caucus.

145. Rossi, Alice S., and Calderwood, Ann, eds. *Academic Women on the Move.* New York: Russell Sage Foundation, 1973.

This is the single most useful source book on the status of academic women from the early 1970s. Among the excellent chapters are contributions devoted to the status of faculty wives at Yale (Myrna M. Weissman et al.); the situation of black women faculty (Constance M. Carroll); the status of women at 145 institutions compared (Lora Robinson); a comparison of women's progress by discipline (Laura Morlock); variations within disciplines by specialty (Michelle Patterson); and the birth and growth of women's studies (Florence Howe and Carol Ahlum). Most pertinent for a consideration of creative approaches to ending sex discrimination are Leonore Weitzmann's chapter on the affirmative action plans in place at forty educational institutions and Margaret Rumbarger's discussion of internal remedies, which includes a model grievance procedure and a review of the role the local chapter of AAUP can play in resolving disputes. Not every piece of statistical evidence is useful. Helen Astin and Allan Bayer did an elaborate multiple regression to demonstrate that the two variables that best predict whether or not an academic is tenured are rank and length of employment.

146. Rossiter, Margaret W. "Sexual Segregation in the Sciences: Some Data and a Model." *Signs: Journal of Women in Culture and Society* 4, 1 (Autumn 1978): 146–51.

This researcher hypothesizes that the growth rate of a field will be linked to the percentage of women in that specialty. Her data show that women's comparative advantage appears to lie at the two extremes in the growth curve. When a field is just being developed or when it is shrinking, the opportunities for women appear to be the best. The model is not perfect, she acknowledges: "Other factors, such as the vast predominance of men, rigid entrance barriers, availability of government employment, or other peculiarities prevent the model which assumes that sexual discrimination is a function of crowding from working more accurately in all fields." Can there by some kind of feedback mechanism that channels women scientists into those fields most open or receptive to them? Not likely, she says, since most vocational guidance steers women toward "safe, familiar 'feminine' fields" and away from "pioneering in risky territory."

147. Rowe, Mary P. "Dealing with Sexual Harassment." *Harvard Business Review* 59, 3 (May-June 1981): 42–46.

Based on her experience mediating cases involving sexual harassment at MIT and other colleges and in industrial organizations, Rowe offers three observations: complainants can be helped to help themselves;

these grievances can usually be resolved through procedures designed to deal with all kinds of complaints, not just those involving sexual harassment; and corporations and universities should confront the issue of power differences in the troubled relationship. Rowe gives specific counsel on ways in which a victim can deal with a harasser—by writing him a letter, for which Rowe provides useful language. She also gives advice on setting up procedures and concludes that "all sexual relationships between supervisors and their subordinates may conflict with company interests." A policy is sometimes helpful to a woman confronted with unwanted sexual advances. She can say, "We can't."

148. **Russell, Michele. "Rapunzel, Let Down Your Hair: An Open Letter to White Women in the Academy."** *College English* 39, 1 (September 1977): 45–52.

This eloquent call to the white women who are now entering academic life in greater numbers says, in essence, "Do not forget your black sisters." "As teachers, scholars, and students, how available will you make your knowledge to others as tools of their own liberation? This is not a call for mindless activism; but, rather, for engaged scholarship."

149. **Safilios-Rothschild, Constantina.** *Sex Role Socialization and Sex Discrimination: A Synthesis and Critique of the Literature.* Washington, D.C.: National Institute of Education, U.S. Department of Health, Education, and Welfare, 1979.

This is 130-page report synthesizing the literature on these topics that appeared between 1960 and 1978. The section on sex discrimination in higher education is short but carefully documented and includes references on studies of graduate student women as well as undergraduates. The major problems these uncovered were lack of women role models, lack of financial aid, unequal admissions policies, and perhaps most serious, lack of encouragement and mentorship by male professors.

150. **Safran, Claire. "Sexual Harassment: The View from the Top."** The joint *Redbook/Harvard Businesss Review* Report: A Survey of 2000 Executives. *Redbook*, March 1981: 45–51.

A 1980 survey of some two thousand subscribers to the *Harvard Business Review* revealed that men and women executives differ in the extent to which they see sexual harassment at work as a problem. Two-thirds of the men, compared to less than one-third of the women, say that the amount of sexual harassment has been "greatly exaggerated." These respondents are compared to the more than nine thousand subscribers to *Redbook* surveyed in 1976, of whom 92 percent described it as a "serious problem." This report describes the executives' views: it includes the tired jokes from men who say they wish they themselves would be harassed and the snippy remarks from women who say it wouldn't be a problem if women dressed and behaved properly. Altogether, a balanced view. The same survey is reported in the *Harvard Business Review* 59, 2 (March-April, 1981) as "Sexual Harassment . . . Some See It. . . . Some Won't" by Eliza G. C. Collins and Timothy B. Blodgett.

151. Schlossberg, Nancy K. "The Right to Be Wrong Is Gone: Women in Academe." *Educational Record* 55, 4 (Fall 1974): 257–62.

The author assesses the situation of women in higher education, noting that the degree aspirations of women have risen at a much sharper rate than those of men but that there are still enormous obstacles in women's way. Among them: internalized barriers, men's attitudes, lack of role models. She ends up musing that if male administrators could only know what it feels like to be a female assistant professor, they might come to understand the feminists' resentment and their sense of urgency.

152. Schumer, Fran R. "A Question of Sex Bias at Harvard." *New York Times Magazine,* October 18, 1981, pp. 96–104.

This is a measured and thoughtful discussion of the complicated case of sociologist Theda Skocpol, who was denied tenure at Harvard in 1980 and dared to charge the department formally with sex discrimination. "One outspoken, ambitious young woman confronted a department of eleven esteemed male sociologists, all of whom considered themselves above the charge of sexism." A committee of three professors from other departments at Harvard reviewed the case and supported Skocpol. This article gives considerable detail about how and why each of the male sociologists voted as they did. The chairman is quoted as saying that she was considered for tenure early, at her own request: "At her urgent request. At her jumping-up-and-down-and-screaming request"—one wonders if he would have chosen that language to describe a male's behavior. Those who voted no on her candidacy were said to be so outraged at the suggestion that they could have discriminated on the basis of sex that the chairman did not even respond to the grievance committee's request for information showing that they had not. The president of the university agreed to reconsider Skocpol in 1984, and she has decided to let the matter rest for the present. In the wake of the uproar, the sociology department at Harvard is now actively seeking women appointees, even as some members still insist that it was her credentials, not her sex, which prompted them to vote against Skocpol.

153. **Simon, Rita James; Clark, Shirley Merritt; and Galway, Kathleen. "The Woman Ph.D.: A Recent Profile."** In *Women and Achievement: Social and Motivational Analyses,* edited by Martha Tamara Shuch Mednick, Sandra Schwartz Tangri, and Lois Wladis Hoffman. New York: John Wiley & Sons, 1975.

This study is based on a sample of 1,764 women who earned their Ph.D.'s between 1958 and 1963 and 492 comparable men. The women differed from the men in marital status: 95 percent of the men were married as compared to 50 percent of the women. Other differences appeared in rank: 46 percent of the men had earned tenure versus 44 percent of the unmarried women, 26 percent of the married women with children, and 22 percent of those women who were married but childless. The authors also conclude that "by various quantitative measures of productivity, the woman Ph.D. publishes as much as her male colleagues (married women, slightly more). . . . " This often quoted article first appeared in *Social Problems* 15, 2 (1969): 221–36.

154. **Simpson, Lawrence Alan.** *Sex Discrimination in the Academic World.* Washington, D.C.: Business and Professional Women's Foundation, 1970.

This six-page publication summarizes the doctoral dissertation written under a grant of the Lena Lake Forrest Fellowship administered by the B & P W Foundation. The researcher sent out identical resumés, some of which described males and others females. His results led him to conclude that "hiring officials do discriminate against women and strongly favor the selection of male faculty. Where qualifications of men and women were equal, substantially more men were chosen."

155. **Speizer, Jeanne J. "Role Models, Mentors, and Sponsors: The Elusive Concepts."** *Signs: Journal of Women in Culture and Society* 6, 4 (Summer 1981): 692–712.

This critical review essay summarizes what is known about the effect of same-sex role models and mentors or sponsors on junior staff and students. The author notes that these concepts have caught the public imagination, but, she says, there is little evidence that women are actually helped by having a woman role model or mentor. Come to that, there is little evidence that men need men in those roles either. The review includes tables summarizing research studies and their results and extremely useful footnotes. The author concludes that strivers might well be less lonely if there were a sufficient number of people like themselves in an organization or educational institution. Increasing the number of women and minorities would ease the pressure on the few there now. This might allow all concerned to "pursue their own goals by trusting in their own competence, unconcerned about whether they have a role model, mentor, or sponsor."

156. **Spriesterbach, D. C., and Farrell, William J. "Impact of Federal Regulations at a University."** *Science* 198, 4312 (October 7, 1977): 27–30.

Studying the costs of implementing federal mandates at six institutions, the authors cite a bill for all of higher education of two billion dollars annually, or roughly the same amount that is received annually from all private sources combined. Major problems include frequent changes in reporting format, different federal agencies imposing different reporting requirements in the same information area, individual reports that duplicate general contract provisions, reports whose costs and complexities far exceed those of comparable reports in the private sector, multiple evaluations of the same activity, reporting requirements unsuited to higher education (for example, regulations based on the assumption that daily attendance is taken in class), and approval or review procedures that involve multiple government units. The opportunity cost of trying to resolve such problems is high, the authors state. Educators should be free to educate. The authors summarize the problem by citing Secretary of Health, Education, and Welfare Califano's comment that most regulations are written as though they were for lawbreakers. The authors call for a renewal of the spirit of partnership and cooperation that once characterized relations between state and gown.

157. **Stoddard, Cynthia, with Little, Antoinette.** *Sex Discrimination in Educational Employment: Legal Alternatives and Strategies.* Holmes Beach, Fla.: Learning Publications, 1981.

This book provides information for women academics on the extent to which they are protected by laws purporting to ensure equal opportunity in educational employment. Chapter IV gives a succinct case study: Ms S is hired by a university at the entry-level position of adjunct professor in 1973 for $13,500. Mr. B, who has identical credentials, is hired six months later at the same level but with a salary of $18,500. S and B are quite good friends; they have known one another since undergraduate days when S tutored B in subjects he found hard. Six years later, B tells S that he has been promoted to tenure, assuming that she has been too. As it develops, she has not. S asks the department head why she had not been advised of the possibility of promotion, and she is given four reasons: (1) B is more qualified; (2) B needs the increased salary; (3) S is pregnant; and (4) there was only one tenured spot open. The author walks us through this complaint, step by laborious step, from filing an internal grievance to getting an attorney to going to state and federal agencies. Stoddard even gives some counsel on how S can retain B's friendship. Filing a suit takes a heavy emotional, mental, and physical toll on a woman who asserts her rights. One hard part, besides the waiting, is that the department chair or dean or whoever is accused of wrongdoing will "defend his innocence to the very end. It would be unusual indeed to have an employer simply agree that he was in fact discriminating against an employee on the basis of sex."

158. **Streckman, Elizabeth K. "I Charged the Government with Sex Discrimination."** *Graduate Woman* 75, 1 (January-February 1981): 8–10.

The grievant recounts, step by step, the struggle of two professional women that took place a decade ago but that has fresh relevance for professionals in higher education. Four well-qualified women were passed over for a new GS-13 opening in favor of a less qualified man. The woman who should have gotten it, identified by the pseudonym Claire Devoe, eventually won the post but only because Streckman had gone to bat for her, paying legal fees and suffering a sad career reversal herself. Devoe never once said thank you—in fact, she was callously unconcerned when the man she had bumped got the job that Streckman was qualified for. Now Streckman takes comfort from the fact that she opened the door for other women to get up to GS-13. She remembers the experience of suing the government in tranquility, but notes wryly that she found herself, at one point, violating the very affirmative action principles she was fighting to establish. That came about when she wrote a job description with a specific candidate in mind: herself. The women she helped were not always grateful for what she did. But, painful as it was, she says she would do it all again.

159. **Stromberg, Ann H., and Harkess, Shirley, eds.** *Women Working: Theories and Facts in Perspective.* Palo Alto, Calif.: Mayfield, 1978.

This book serves as an excellent introduction to the general study of women's work in America. Two sections are of special interest to those concerned with problems of sex discrimination in higher education: chapter 12, in which Michelle Patterson and Laurie Engelberg describe the problems encountered by women in male-dominated professions, including college teaching, and chapter 18, in which Constantina Safilios-Rothschild analyzes the implications of the evidence for policy change. Among the topics she analyzes are the "all or nothing" model of achievement and employment and the "normalization of the dual-work family." A particularly interesting passage has to do with the "cold war" against successful women and how peace can be brought about.

160. **Tavris, Carol, and Offir, Carole.** *The Longest War: Sex Differences in Perspective.* New York: Harcourt Brace Jovanovich, 1977.

This book differs from most texts in that it is lively as well as literate. It summarizes scholarly approaches to the study of sex differences in useful sections: the biological perspective, the psychoanalytic perspective, the sociological, learning, and evolutionary perspectives—and there is even an instructive section on international comparisons. The passage most pertinent to female academics is called "Work: Opportunity, Power, and Tokenism." Especially interesting is the discussion of the effects on the all-male group of having a sole woman team member and the effects (insofar as we know them) on the lone female herself.

161. **Tidball, M. Elizabeth. "Perspective on Academic Women and Affirmative Action."** *Educational Record* 54, 2 (Spring 1973): 130–35.

Affirmative action appears to be working nicely for women students, this author observes, in that the formerly all-male fields of study and institutions are becoming integrated. But, she says, "one cannot expect a high return on the investment in women students if institutions are uncommitted or hostile to women academic professionals." Analyzing a sample of 1,500 whose biographies have appeared in *Who's Who of American Women,* Tidball concludes that women's colleges are significantly more likely to have produced women of high achievement—as measured by inclusion in *Who's Who*—than coeducational institutions. She shows this in turn to be related to the presence of women faculty: "the number of women faculty and the number of women achievers were highly and positively correlated." Finally, she notes, the number of women faculty in all undergraduate educational institutions has been declining for the last forty years. Those two findings taken together do not augur well for women either as students or faculty. Some have criticized her study as having a faulty measurement of achievement or leadership, but few have challenged her basic premise that women students can surely profit from having role models of both sexes.

162. **Tidball, M. Elizabeth, and Kistiakowsky, Vera. "Baccalaureate Origins of American Scientists and Scholars."** *Science* 193, 4254 (August 20, 1976): 646–52.

In the past, these authors observe, institutions of higher education seldom found it "necessary or useful to examine themselves for evidence of policies or attitudes that affect women and men differentially." Now, with the passage of federal antibias regulations, there may be more interest in studies such as the one reported here. Analyzing data from the Doctorate Records File since 1920, the authors found that undergraduate institutions that graduated large numbers and high percentages of women who went on to earn the Ph.D. differed quite markedly from institutions that produced high numbers of men who went on to earn doctorates. Women Ph.D.'s came from institutions that enrolled large numbers of women, had long and continuous histories of women graduates earning doctorates, and offered strong academic preparation in several different areas. Men, in contrast, came from institutions with a high proportion of male students and a focus on a narrow range of academic interests. Among the most productive institutions of women scholars: the Seven Sisters, University of Chicago, and Cornell University. It should be added that the latter two were also very productive of women who were highly vocal about the need for change in the late 1960s and early 1970s.

163. **Van Alstyne, Carol; Withers, Julie; and Elliott, Sharon. "Affirmative Inaction: The Bottom Line Tells the Tale."** *Change* 9, 8 (August 1977): 39.

The College and University Personnel Association surveyed member institutions in the academic year 1975–76; 38 percent of them were willing to provide the requested data about the race and sex of their administrators. Studying 18,035 administrators in fifty-two carefully specified job titles at 1,037 institutions, the authors found 79 percent were white men; 14 percent white women; 5 percent minority men; and less than 2 percent minority women. An additional finding: "Salary differentials among administrators holding equivalent jobs at peer institutions were far more closely related to sex than to race. Women were paid only about 80 percent of the going rate for men. Minority men were paid about the same as white men in equivalent jobs." Only one administrative position of the fifty-two studied had a sizable representation of all four race and sex groups: the affirmative action-equal opportunity officer. In this post, white men and minority men earned more than women; minority women earned 7 percent less than men and white women 12 percent less.

164. **Vanderwaerdt, Lois. "Higher Education Discrimination and the Courts."** *Journal of Law and Education* 10, 4 (October 1981):467–83.

This pithy article, by an attorney who is both assistant professor of business law and director of affirmative action at the University of Missouri–St. Louis, presents persuasive evidence that judges are willing to review personnel decisions affecting lawyers, physicians, managers, and secondary school teachers much more willingly than decisions affecting college professors. Reviewing the case of *Johnson* v. *University of Pittsburgh* (see table 2), Vanderwaerdt notes that the judge upheld the department's right to ignore the quality of the plaintiff's research if that work was deemed to be irrelevant to the department's mission. Furthermore, the judge wrote, the department was not required to appraise her of the fact that her research did not fit their needs until the final decision on her candidacy for tenure. In other words, Vanderwaerdt writes, while industrial organizations have to demonstrate that their promotion criteria are significantly related to performance, colleges do not. Similarly, the courts have paid far less attention to the absence of demographic peers among evaluators at colleges than elsewhere, have weighed statistics showing underrepresentation differently in academic and industrial cases, and have permitted attorneys in industry (but not in college) cases to have access to confidential documents. But a new line of decisions, Vanderwaerdt says, holds promise for extending the protection of Title VII to academic women: *Sweeney* v. *Keene State College, Jepsen* v. *Florida Board of Regents,* and *Kunda* v. *Muhlenberg College* (see table 2). These, plus voluntary efforts on campus to change both official processes and subtler practices may provide an equality in employment "not yet seen for women and minorities in academe."

165. **Vetter, Betty M. "Working Women Scientists and Engineers."** *Science* 207, 4426 (January 4, 1980): 28–34.

Studying the results of several different surveys of women scientists and engineers, the author concludes that much better data are needed before an accurate statistical portrait of their economic and professional characteristics can be presented. Different researchers analyze the same data quite differently, she notes, and naturally draw different conclusions. She does feel that it is clear that policy changes would make the path of the woman scientist easier. Major barriers have been removed, but the ones that remain "are not easily remedied because they are subtle." She calls for programs for women who have taken career breaks and need to reenter scientific and technological fields; for financial aid for part-time as well as full-time students; and for increased opportunities for part-time work. About 80 percent of women trained in science or engineering are in the labor force, she notes, but many are employed outside their fields. Of women with doctorates in science or engineering, between 89.5 and 96.0 percent are in the labor force, so the educational investment is clearly not wasted.

166. **Vladeck, Judith P., and Young, Margaret M. "Sex Discrimination in Higher Education: It's Not Academic."** *Women's Rights Law Reporter* 4, 2 (Winter 1978): 59–78.

This landmark article was among the first to summarize the effect on academic women of the passage of Title VII. It was passed from hand to hand at women's conferences in the late 1970s as a vital resource. The authors say that the legislative history of the 1972 amendments makes clear that Congress intended to end the exemption of colleges and universities as a class of employers who could pursue policies otherwise prohibited by law. But problems arose. Judges proved to be reluctant to intervene in what they perceived to be the domain of academics and, further, hostile to women who charged their colleagues with sex discrimination. The authors spell out how plaintiffs can establish a prima facie case for the existence of sex discrimination on their campuses, discuss the definition of and need for class action suits, and outline the need for statistical proof of the underrepresentation of women in high-level posts in universities. But, they conclude, "the most carefully presented statistics may not persuade a judge who does not wish to be persuaded. Faculty women need to help in the education process of the judiciary." An equally useful update appeared in the Spring 1978 issue of *Women's Rights Law Reporter*.

167. **Vowels, Robert C. "Professional Research on Minority Economic Problems and Its Effect on Academic Hiring."** *American Journal of Economics and Scoiology* 38, 1:(January 1979): 61–72.

The author reviewed articles (including reviews and comments) that focused on minority economic problems and appeared in any of twenty-nine major economic journals between 1970 and 1976. He compared their career profile characteristics with those of economists who had chosen other economic specialities. The number of articles on minority economic problems, especially those linked to labor and manpower problems, increased substantially during the period studied. These tended to be written by economists from high-prestige institutions. The author concludes that "institutional relationships and an economics-journal-communications network effectively influenced the hiring of the economists studied. In 1970–76 the highest hiring frequencies were for economists with Ph.D.s from their own prestige-type universities and publishing in the prestige journals on minority economic problems."

168. **Wagner, Lawrence D. "Tenure and Promotion in Higher Education in Light of Washington v. Davis."** *Wayne Law Review* 24, 1–2 (1977–78): 95–132.

Since it is harder to prove discrimination in a Title VII case brought by an individual than in a class action, this author says, it is important that college teachers be able to take advantage of the option to have their grievances framed as class actions. A class action is no less proper for professionals than for others, he holds, and hails the *Mecklenburg* v. *Montana State University* decision as a long overdue step forward. "While disparities per se are not illegal, it was their existence more so than 'isolated acts' of discrimination that prompted passage of much of the civil rights legislation. In a sense then, it is only proper that the beneficiaries of that legislation use disparities to help put a halt to the employment discrimination present today in higher education."

169. **Wasserman, Elga; Lewin, Arie Y.; and Bleiweis, Linda H., eds.** *Women in Academia: Evolving Policies toward Equal Opportunities.* New York: Praeger, 1975.

This important book is introduced with a statement that there is overwhelming evidence that "women faculty are evaluated on the basis of different criteria at the time of the hiring decision." Real progress, the editors note, can be measured only by an increased ratio of women to men in the tenured ranks. Therefore, affirmative action is needed; its success will depend on the "commitment, energy, and courage of those faculty members and administrators in a position to influence recruitment, hiring, and admissions policies. . . . " The volume includes articles by Bernice Sandler, Lilli Hornig (on "affirmative attitudes"), Mary I. Bunting (on creating opportunities for women in science), and interesting case histories about affirmative action efforts at Carnegie-Mellon University and Stanford. Also included is Alice H. Cook's article reviewed elsewhere in this bibliography. The editors assert that "an analysis of the material in this volume should clarify the widespread misunderstanding about preferential hiring, reverse discrimination, goals and quotas, and the alleged need to lower academic hiring standards in order to achieve equity based on sex and race." (See also *Cook, Alice H.*)

170. **Wehrwein, Austin C. "Sex-Bias Claims Filed in Minnesota."** *Chronicle of Higher Education* 21, 22 (February 9, 1981): 10.

At least sixteen sex discrimination claims have been filed against the University of Minnesota as a result of the August 1980 consent decree signed by the institution and plaintiff Shyamala Rajender, according to this report. Rajender's lawyers estimate that settlement could cost as much as $60 million; and "Charles May, the university's lawyer, estimated the maximum benefit to female faculty members and job applicants at about $735,000 over the life of the decree." This reporter notes that Brown University has been under a less sweeping consent decree since 1977. Brown set up a fund of $400,000 to satisfy any judgments resulting from the decree; a total of $107,000 was awarded. "Overall, Brown spent $1.1 million, including about $1 million in lawyers' fees."

171. **Weisberg, D. Kelly. "Women in Law School Teaching: Problems and Progress."** *Journal of Legal Education* 30, 1–2 (1979): 226–48.

In 1972, the Association of American Law Schools adopted a resolution at its annual meeting that "all law schools should . . . make substantial efforts to recruit, hire, and promote women professors." Since that time, little progress appears to have been made. By 1976, women constituted 7.9 percent of all law faculty in member schools, averaging 4.8 percent in the largest, and most prestigious, law schools. Of the 310 women law professors, 25 are law librarians. The author's research identified 5 women deans. Why so few in the faculty? Weisberg lists many possible explanations: the fact that there is discrimination; the difficulty of managing family and career; the fact that women may not be going to the most prestigious law schools to which they can be admitted but rather studying where their husbands or boyfriends are; the fact that many law faculties require that candidates have held clerkships in federal court, posts which were more difficult for women to get, regardless of their merit; the fact that editorships of law reviews are a qualification highly valued and that these too often were more difficult for women than men; women's exclusion from the old-boy network; and finally the fact that for women, an additional criterion seems to be important—good looks. One woman who was editor of her law review and first in her class was turned down for an academic appointment because as one faculty member said, "I can't work with anyone that ugly."

172. **Weisstein, Naomi. "'How Can a Little Girl Like You Teach a Great Big Class of Men?' the Chairman Said, and Other Adventures of a Woman in Science."** In *Working It Out: Twenty-three Women Writers, Artists, Scientists, and Scholars Talk about their Lives and Work,* edited by Sara Ruddick and Pamela Daniels. New York: Pantheon, 1977.

This is a personal account by an experimental psychologist who encountered deep prejudice against women graduate students and beginning professionals. As an undergraduate at Wellesley, she had been warned that academic men would not like her competing with them. But she did not recognize the reality that women were not welcome in psychology until the first day of her graduate work at Harvard. A star professor puffed on his pipe and told the assembly of incoming students that women do not belong in graduate school. She could not believe her ears. But she fought such attitudes and continues to. An unusual aspect of this account is the author's willingness to name names.

173. **WEOUP (Women for Equal Opportunity at the University of Pennsylvania).** Minutes. Philadelphia, Pa.: Penn Women's Center, University of Pennsylvania.

The minutes of the meetings of this group are the most avidly read of any at the University of Pennsylvania, according to Helen Davies, associate professor of microbiology, in the school of medicine there. Women faculty, administrators, staff, and students are all welcome in this group. Anyone off campus who would care to receive copies of the minutes by joining WEOUP is invited to write to the organization. There is special interest at Penn in coalitions with campus women's groups elsewhere.

174. **Westervelt, Esther M.** *"Opportunities for Women in Higher Education: Their Current Participation, Prospects for the Future, and Recommendations for Action: A Report and Recommendations by the Carnegie Commission on Higher Education,"* Harvard Educational Review 44, 2 (May 1974): 295–313.

Westervelt found the Carnegie Commission report, which aimed to achieve maximum gains for women at minimum cost to the institution, to favor institutions over women. Its five recommendations—establishment of goals and timetables, availability of part-time appointments, maternity leave, abolition of antinepotism rules, and establishment of internal grievance procedures—are, she notes, measures required by affirmative action guidelines. Such recommendations are well within institutional feasibility but hardly enough to satisfy the most activist women's groups—or to bring about rapid change. She found the commission report quite conservative. Nevertheless, she notes, the report does represent a milestone in the history of women in higher education: "the point at which a group clearly identified with the establishment accepted the authenticity of women's demands for equality."

175. **Widom, Cathy Spatz, and Burke, Barbara W.** "Performance, Attitudes, and Professional Socialization of Women in Academia." *Sex Roles* 4, 4 (1978): 549–62.

The authors compared 126 untenured faculty members at two colleges in the Northwest in terms of their responses to a questionnaire on their achievement and attitudes toward their work. Among the questions were items about the number and type of publications the faculty member had and how he or she would rank his or her reputation. The men's self-ranking appeared to correspond to their publication rate; the women's did not. There was a clear sex difference between the sexes in publication rate but an even greater difference in faculty members at the two colleges; that is, women at college A published less than men at college A but more than men at college B, who in turn published more than women at college B. Thus, the authors conclude, situation is more important than sex. The researchers find a suggestion in their data that women appear to direct their efforts in areas that are not necessarily rewarded.

176. **Winkler, Karen J.** "Women Historians Have Greater Access to Some Jobs but Remain Concentrated in 'Underpaid Ranks.'" *Chronicle of Higher Education* 21, 18 (January 12, 1981): 8.

A report on the status of women in the historical profession was presented to the American Historical Association at its annual meetings. The statistics and other evidence support the conclusion cited in the title of this summary article. Of all men receiving the Ph.D. in history between 1970 and 1974, one-third were full professors by 1980; in contrast, of the women earning doctorates in history during the same period, fewer than one-eighth were full professors by 1980. Studying the next cohort, those earning history doctorates between 1975 and 1978, the researchers found that 27 percent of the men—versus 9 percent of the women—had reached the rank of associate professor by the end of the decade. Fewer than 10 percent of the male historians were in dead-end teaching posts; over 30 percent of the women were stalled there. There are more women historians teaching and doing research in academic institutions in 1980 than previously, but as one women noted, "there is a proletariat being created in the professoriate—and it is female."

177. **Wolfe, Julie C.; DeFleur, Melvin L.; and Slocum, Walter L.** "Sex Discrimination in Hiring Practices of Graduate Sociology Departments: Myths and Realities." *American Sociologist* 8 (November 1973): 159–68.

These researchers present data that they believe shows that the major cause of the underrepresentation of women in graduate sociology departments is the lack of women sociologists with the Ph.D.: " . . . this disparity rather than prejudicial staffing practices as such, . . . requires our greatest attention." They conclude that more women need to be encouraged to undertake graduate work in sociology. In the comment that follows the article, the members of the American Sociological Association Committee on the Status of Women in Sociology review the data and find them inadequate to support the authors' conclusions. Women earned 25 percent of the Ph.D.'s awarded in sociology in 1969–70, but comprised only 12 percent of those hired by graduate departments of sociology that year. In the same issue, the authors add a response to their critics calling for more research on the unemployed Ph.D. women, to find out why they are not working, a proposal that nobody could take issue with. This is a classic exchange, with the original authors saying only a quarter of the Ph.D.'s go to women and therefore we need more, and their critics saying fully a quarter are women, of whom half aren't hired.

178. **Young, Margaret Moses. "Sex Discrimination in Higher Education: Women's Work."** Civil Liberties Review 5, 2 (July-August 1978): 41–43.

Despite the clear Congressional mandate, the courts have been loath to take a close look at university employment practices. There are two attitudinal problems here, this author says: male judges do not seem to be willing to look at sex discrimination cases, and the courts have "accepted the premise that colleges and universities operate on a system of unrestricted meritocracy where rewards are doled out according to judgments made by those most qualified to do so." With regard to the first, she notes that in a recent sex discrimination case brought by a faculty member against the University of Maryland, the judge went so far as to comment in front of the jury that the suit did not belong in court, and that perhaps sex bias laws should not be on the books. Young cites a recent First Circuit Court of Appeals decision to deplore the hands-off policy, and she urges other courts to follow suit. "Failure to do so will mean that academic women have been singled out as a group which, unlike almost all other kinds of employees, has no recourse under law for sex discrimination."

179. **Yurko, Richard J. "Judicial Recognition of Academic Collective Interests: A New Approach to Faculty Title VII Litigation."** Boston University Law Review 60, 3 (1980): 473–541.

Attorney Yurko takes us back to 1790, to the first suit brought against an American educational institution and brings us to the present, showing that, since 1950, there has been a 500 percent increase in suits brought by faculty against their employers. But most plaintiffs lose because of a "classic problem of circularity. Academic institutions are accorded judicial deference unless a plaintiff can prove discrimination, but few plaintiffs can prove discrimination because academic institutions are accorded judicial deference." How can individual faculty members' civil rights be protected? Yurko proposes that courts must recognize the collective interests of all faculty members and practice only qualified, informed deference, based in part on an understanding of an individual institution's mission. His examples are instructive; his arguments are persuasive. His compromise represents a creative approach to resolving sex-based employment disputes in that it recognizes both the power of the law and its limitations and the important principle that colleges and universities must be preserved as entities distinct from government, including the judiciary.

General Index

The numbers in roman type refer to entry numbers.
The numbers in italic type refer to page numbers.

Index to Coauthors, Coeditors, and Editors